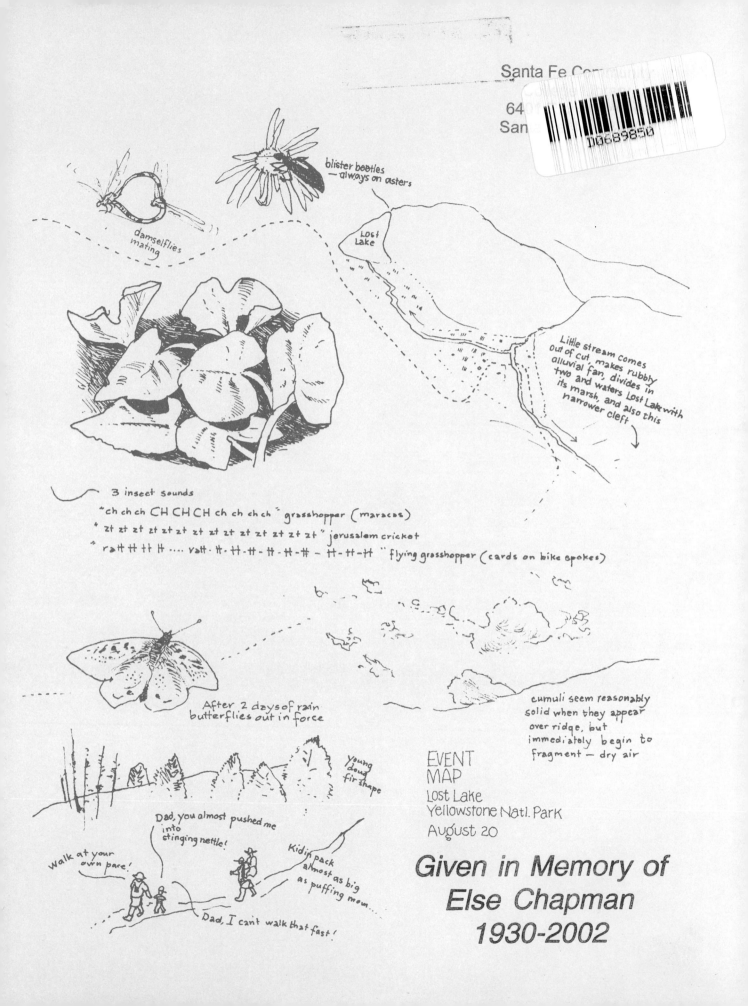

blister beetles
— always on asters

damselflies
mating

Lost
Lake

Little stream comes
out of cut makes rubbly
alluvial fan, divides in
two and waters Lost Lake with
its marsh, and also this
narrower cleft

3 insect sounds

"ch ch ch CH CH CH ch ch ch ch" grasshopper (maracas)

"zt zt zt zt zt zt zt zt zt zt zt zt zt zt" jerusalem cricket

"ratt tt tt tt .... ratt - tt - tt - tt - tt - tt - tt - tt - tt - tt" flying grasshopper (cards on bike spokes)

After 2 days of rain
butterflies out in force

cumuli seem reasonably
solid when they appear
over ridge, but
immediately begin to
fragment — dry air

Young doug
fir shape

EVENT
MAP
Lost Lake
Yellowstone Natl. Park
August 20

Dad, you almost pushed me
into
stinging nettle!

Walk at your
own pace!

Kid's pack
almost as big
as puffing mom...

Dad, I cant walk that fast!

also by Hannah Hinchman

A Life in Hand:
Creating the Illuminated Journal

A Trail Through Leaves

The Journal as a Path to Place

A Trail Through Leaves

THE JOURNAL AS A PATH TO PLACE

Hannah Hinchman

W · W · NORTON & COMPANY · NEW YORK · LONDON

Copyright © 1997 by Hannah Hinchman

For information about permission to reproduce selections from this book, write to Permissions, W. W. Norton & Company, Inc., 500 Fifth Avenue, New York, NY 10110.

The text of this book is composed in Centaur
with the display set in Koch Antiqua
Composition by Antonina Krass
Manufacturing by South China Printing Co. Ltd.
Book design by Antonina Krass

Library of Congress Cataloging-in-Publication Data

Hinchman, Hannah.
A trail through leaves : the journal as a path to place / Hannah Hinchman.
p. cm.

ISBN 0-393-04101-8

1. Natural history—Authorship.   2. Diaries—Authorship.
I. Title.
QH14.H46   1997
808' .066508—dc21   96-37100
CIP

W. W. Norton & Company, Inc., 500 Fifth Avenue, New York, N.Y. 10110
http://www.wwnorton.com

W. W. Norton & Company Ltd., 10 Coptic Street, London WC1A 1PU

1 2 3 4 5 6 7 8 9 0

For M. B. G. L.

CONTENTS

A Trail Through Leaves

THE JOURNAL AS A PATH TO PLACE

IN
A
WYOMING
GARDEN

Chapter 1

GOING TO THE SOURCE

When I began my first journal, I meant it to be a volume of woods lore, based on Ernest Thomson Seton's *Two Little Savages*, his illustrated volume of life in the wild. My northwoods at the time (I was 17) was a 300-acre nature center, once a prosperous Ohio farm, that I had adopted as my true home. Whenever I could be spared from answering the phones and selling field guides and bird feeders at the nature center store, I'd take that scuffed little black book (titled "Hannah H., Her Life and Times", Volume One) and my latest rapidograph pen, and go out walking on Aullwood's mown trails, through maturing deciduous woods, beside a little creek, and across a replanted prairie opening. Sometimes the day stewed in Midwestern mugginess, and I'd be baffled to find that I wasn't rapturous, but only hot, itchy, and dull-witted. Other times I felt that I had stepped into the Garden of Eden, and resented the occasional herd of noisy schoolkids, from whom I hid.

At least once a week, much to my parents' bewilderment, I'd get up long before dawn to drive through downtown in my lumbering, nearly brakeless '53 Willy's jeep, arriving at Aullwood while it was still dark. I wanted to hear every note of the predawn bird chorus, wanted to catch the last pocket of night-air fragrance, wanted to see what the sun would make of the wash of dew on everything.

Before I closed the covers on Volume One, I had discovered that the journal was my most powerful ally in crafting the kind of life I wanted. I was building a scaffolding of choices and attitudes, forging affinities, discovering what colors, places, times of the day I could truly call "mine." This self-definition played out against a background of romanticism and idealism, in the voices of William Wordsworth, Ralph Waldo Emerson, and William Cullen Bryant. I combed books of poetry, copying page upon page of it into my little

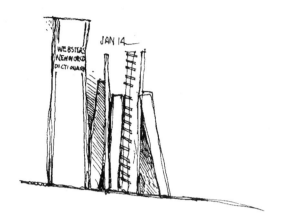

black book, shoring up the self-under-construction with what seemed to me to be the finest possible materials.

I memorized passages that could have been written for the reawakening of the environmental movement in the seventies: "The world is too much with us; late and soon,/Getting and spending, we lay waste our powers:/Little we see in Nature that is ours;/We have given our hearts away, a sordid boon!" Transcribing *Tintern Abbey* allowed it to imprint my moldable soul, sentiments and speech patterns both.

And yet practical matters found their way into the pages, too: How could I fulfill my destiny as a naturalist if I couldn't abide noisy schoolkids? And suffered from debilitating stage-fright if I had to talk to more than one person at a time? And what else was I suited to be? I could barely make change at the nature center store. An indifferent student, I knew I was hewing a future from the rawest of raw material. In those first few volumes, I tended to write manifestos and resolutions: "I am looking for true, soul-filled experience, the motive behind my wanting to live in a cabin in the woods, grow my own food and listen to country-gutsy music, etc. I'm tired of glossy, retouched, plastic, overdubbed, laughtracked, advertised experience. I want crude —straight from the soul." It seemed a good idea to be a mystical savage for awhile.

Planning elaborate outdoor adventures required more adult skills than anything my high school demanded of me. I leapt into my first canoeing and camping trips with an organized fury, sometimes alone, sometimes with friends, only a few of whom seemed to grasp the enormous portent of what we were doing. I tried to make sure that these

THE TURNIP-FARMER ROSE AND WITH A FRESH PULLED TURNIP... POINTED TO MY ROAD
— ISSA

We rouse ourselves and make a fire, the best way to become fully awake and ready for a day.

Smells of woodsmoke and pancakes are especially noticeable to my innocent morning senses.

grand embarkations into the heart of nature weren't tainted by the prosaic, insisting on imagining that we were dressed in buckskin loincloths instead of flannel shirts and blue jeans, and cooking in buffalo paunches instead of army surplus mess kits. I wanted these first adventures to form an unassailable world, composed only of pure things. I courted the idea of miracles, of impossible meetings with animals, messages passing between us. Without the journal, none of this would have seemed so momentous. With it, I was able to keep on believing in the newness of the world.

At the time, I favored floor-length, old-fashioned dresses, and wore them even to school: a mistaken attempt to carry a secret world into the larger one. But a perfect place to wear those gowns presented itself right about then—another old Ohio farm, bought by the county park system to recreate a farm from the 1850s, where I volunteered to be the woman who baked bread in a Dutch oven. Ironically, that task kindled a latent domesticity unaroused by any high school Home Ec. class, and in answering the visitors' questions, I learned that I could speak without getting tongue-tied. While the bread baked under its coal-laden lid, I ran out to the big old barn and danced Virginia reels to the music of the Hot Mud Family.

And I maintained the search for that mysterious

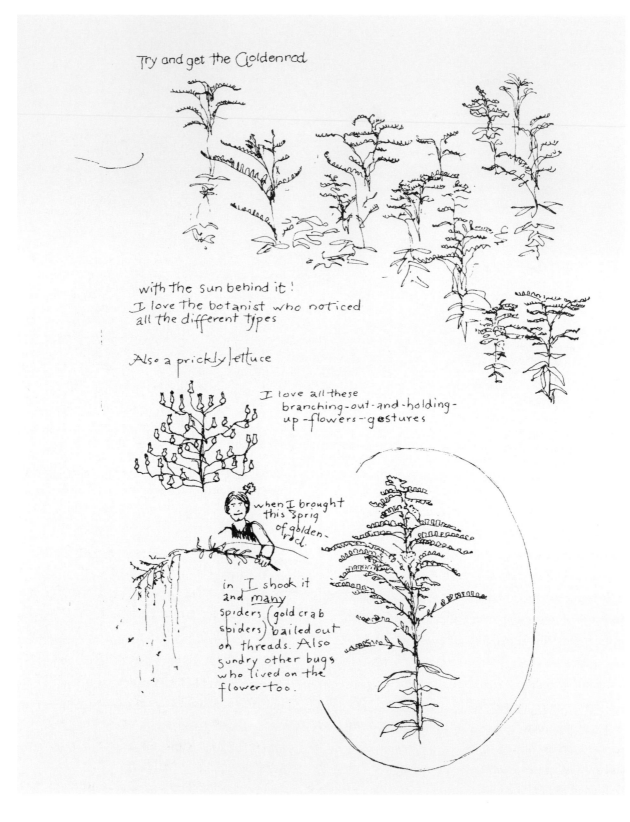

Try and get the Goldenrod

with the sun behind it!
I love the botanist who noticed
all the different types

Also a prickly lettuce

I love all these
branching-out-and-holding-
up-flowers-gestures

when I brought
this sprig
of golden-
rod.

in, I shook it
and *many*
spiders (gold crab
spiders) bailed out
on threads. Also
sundry other bugs
who lived on the
flower too.

thing, "a presence that disturbs my mind with the joy of elevated thought," as Wordsworth described it. It was most potently present at dawn and dusk, and almost too real at night: for years I was terrified of being in the woods in the dark. I thought of this presence as a spring that flowed only intermittently; I couldn't will it into being and couldn't predict where I'd find it. When other people were present, it retreated, no matter how reverent our attitude. It was the source of a nameless sweetness, and I wanted to be near it.

And in the plain daylight it also withdrew, so I simply waited and soaked up atmospheres, the hot, rank herbaceous smell of the meadows (the strongest smell came from Queen-Anne's lace) that went with the indolent songs of wood pewees and red-eyed vireos in the second growth woods that edged, and edged into, the meadows. The acridity of black walnuts, red cedars, and osage orange fruits. The fungoid heady scent of leaf mold; the grotesque rottery of methane mud on the edges of ponds. All of these things were signs of the mysterious source.

And then there was the "ancient" smell I've still

never been able to trace, that emanated just as the air began to cool after sundown in early spring. It smelled of old wood, earth, and books, but suggested much more than that, and carried a kind of sadness or yearning, a nostalgia for the passing moment. In cold spring dusks in the back pastures of abandoned Ohio farms, waiting for the woodcocks to begin their mating dance, I'd tramp along the old fencerows, confused by the emotions that came with that scent, feeling like an old soul bidding farewell to everything dear. That youthful sadness sometimes brought me close to the nameless presence, which didn't belong only to the glad moments, but was intimately bound up with attachment and loss as well.

There were rituals, enacted with utter earnestness. I didn't feel that I had created them, but that they had existed for eons and I'd somehow become an initiate. In late May I'd begin listening for the first wood thrush, my totem animal before I understood the word "totem." I dressed in my idea of a wood-nymph gown to seek it, stealing out at dawn, playing a certain song on the soprano recorder, crowned with a wreath of bedstraw and trillium. Hearing the first strains of the wood thrush each spring was an act of apotheosis. One morning, though, after a heavy rain, I stood on a log over a swollen creek to listen: no thrush. And the creek carried raw sewage from the new subdivisions now corraling it.

9·10
Remembering
with pleasure
this wide bowl
of sound (nutcracker
wingbeats, thunk of
horses' hooves in a
trailer, far off raven
cry, rider with one
pack horse crossing
a bridge over a
marshy place)
light & ramparts
of Holmsian Absaroka
cliffs.
Clouds, however,
spell a high-level
disturbance
(jet contrails
persisting, spreading)
3 quiet hikers.
Wind way over there.
Chickadee calls

Sunflower bed
beneath Shirley's
windows

One day each summer would be selected for its perfection; to celebrate it required abandoning all other plans to spend the entire day afield. In autumn, the festival coincided with Thanksgiving, and involved packing a feast of nuts, fruit, grain, sunflower seeds, and suet into the woods for the animals, to be deposited with the reading of a poem ("Oh ye blessed creatures, I hear the calls ye to each other make . . .") and a song, the old hymn "How Can I Keep from Singing?" The notion of a feast for the animals came from a book I loved as a child: *Rabbit Hill* by Robert Lawson.

Writing about these solitary passionate acts now, twenty-five years later, I'm embarrassed by them, but also queerly moved. The structure I created for myself in those years, and fiercely defended, and retreated to in times of trouble (and plenty of that came later) actually did prove to be the foundation of my life, and not simply an adolescent fancy. At the time, the motivations were partly rebellion and withdrawal: I felt that I was grow-

ing up too fast, I didn't understand the implications of sex and power the way other girls my age appeared to (at least they were able to manipulate them far better than I could). I wanted a way out, I needed a private sanctuary. I wanted to stay by the wellspring and not have to grapple with the sordid, the treacherous, the spiteful.

For a while that is how it worked, but as a gregarious rather than a monk-like kid, one whose hormones kept impelling her into the arms of the projected hero, I couldn't maintain my sanctuary in its purity. Journal entries about walks in the woods are increasingly interrupted by romantic reveries: Will Chris come over tonight and should I be wearing my wood nymph gown? Still, I realized the danger of depending too much on a boy's approval, knew that it would compromise my self-creation, and fought those dependent tendencies with impassioned prose in the journal. I have a strong affection for that fierce girl who created a world.

Sometimes I think she is lost forever. Is it because I no longer have the Peter Pan-like power simply to *believe*? Breaking through to the wellspring requires a certain kind of cultivation now. It is an intentional act of recovering innocence. A great weight of sadness accumulates over the years, building up like travertine hot-spring deposits on the original bedrock of wonder. Enchantment is burdened by disappointment, unfulfilled promises, exhaustion, cruelty, the shackles of habit. And yet even the first journal, and the awakening it was meant to record, was undertaken deliberately. It was a prescient attempt to preserve innocence.

In subsequent journals, the wood-nymph persona with her costumes and rituals became less necessary to me, while her openness and curiosity

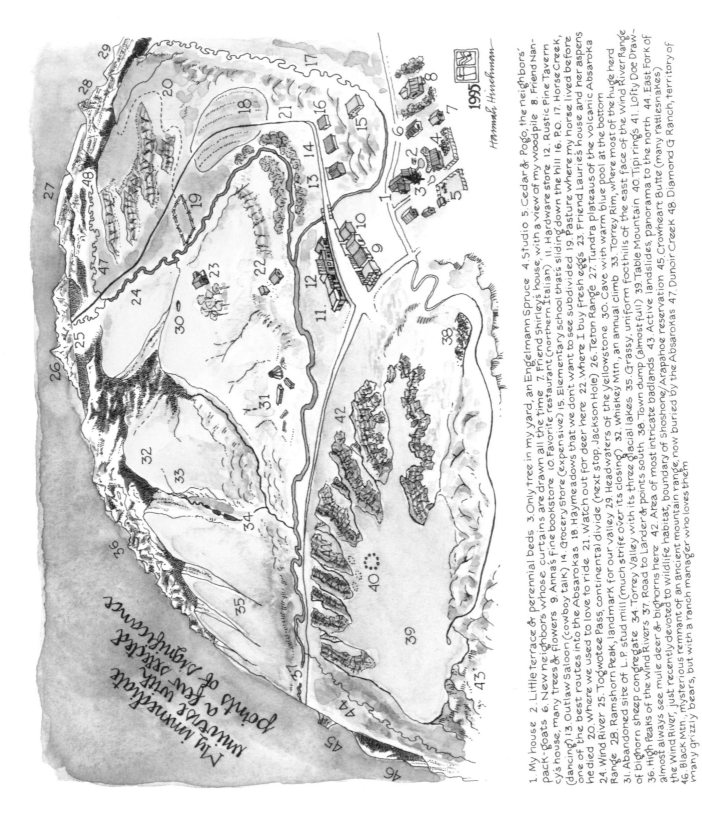

My immediate universe with a few scribbled points of insignificance

1. My house 2. Little terrace & perennial beds 3. Only tree in my yard, an Engelmann Spruce 4. Studio 5. Cedar & Pogo, the neighbors' pack-goats 6. New neighbors whose curtains are drawn all the time 7. Friend Shirley's house, with a view of my woodpile 8. Friend Nancy's house 9. Anna's fine bookstore 10. Favorite restaurant (northern Italian) 11. Hardware store 12. Rustic Pine Tavern (dancing) 13. Outlaw Saloon (cowboy talk) 14. Grocery Store (expensive) 15. Elementary school that's sliding down the hill 16. P.O. 17. Horse Creek, one of the best routes into the Absarokas 18. Haymeadows that we don't want to see subdivided 19. Pasture where my horse lived before he died 20. where we used to love to ride 21. Watch out for deer here 22. where I buy fresh eggs 23. Friend Laurie's house and her aspens 24. Wind River 25. Togwotee Pass, continental divide (next stop, Jackson Hole) 26. Teton Range 27. Tundra plateaus of the volcanic Absaroka Range 28. Ramshorn Peak, landmark for our valley 29. Headwaters of the Yellowstone 30. Cave with warm blue pool at the bottom 31. Abandoned site of L.P. stud mill (much strife over its closing) 32. Whiskey Mtn., an annual climb 33. Torrey Rim, where most of the Wind River Range of bighorn sheep congregate 34. Torrey Valley with its three glacial lakes 35. Grassy, uniform foothills of the east face of the Wind River Range 36. High Peaks of the Wind Rivers 37. Road to Lander & points south 38. Town dump (almost full) 39. Table Mountain 40. Tipi rings 41. Lofty Doe Draw—almost always see mule deer & bighorns here 42. Area of most intricate badlands 43. Active landslides, panorama to the north 44. East Fork of the Wind River, just recently devoted to wildlife habitat, boundary of Shoshone/Arapahoe reservation 45. Crowheart Butte (many rattlesnakes) 46. Black Mtn., mysterious remnant of an ancient mountain range, now buried by the Absarokas 47. Dunoir Creek 48. Diamond G Ranch, territory of many grizzly bears, but with a ranch manager who loves them

Hannah Hinchman

1995

persisted and became the core of a more mature personality. In the early volumes I knew nothing about the patterns of fear, mistrust, withdrawal, and weakness that would surge upward to sabotage love affairs and a marriage, and prevent steady artistic growth. They might have done more damage if a strong link to the world hadn't been formed early—a link in which the landscape, the doings of creatures and plants and weather could, and still can, penetrate bleak feelings of unworthiness and uselessness. If I were about to pull the trigger and happened to hear a red-winged blackbird, I doubt that I could complete the act.

Like so many nomadic kids of my era, I found my way to the West, after summers of backpacking there during college. One look at Wyoming and I was ready to leave everything familiar without a backward glance, and did, with a detour to Maine for art school. Now it's twenty years later, and I'm still here, learning late about what it means to live in a "community." I would have scoffed at the idea until a few years ago, preferring to believe that, though I might live in a town, I wasn't of it.

I should have guessed what a nester I was at heart, carrying my books, art supplies, and collections of feathers and stones from dwelling to dwelling, setting up a little shrine of treasured objects in each of them, be it tipi or apartment, twenty-seven "homes" in all. And that I would actually enjoy and thrive in the close-knit human relationships of a small town, relishing the eccentricities and quirks of its residents, and knowing that I'm firmly embedded as one of them.

Now I finally have a real home, a little house in this tiny western town ringed by mountains. It's what you'd have to call decrepit, sagging and listing, but it has charm. One part of it is built of huge old logs, hand-hewn by Scandinavians who cut railroad ties from the surrounding forests (the logs were covered up by fake wood paneling when I bought the place). The other part is flimsy frame with tired insulation and single-pane windows, built, I suspect, by some harried father on weekends. The stairs are strange: toward the top the risers get higher and the treads narrower, as though the builder's calculations had been off from the bottom up. And there really isn't enough space in the roof peak to accommodate a second story, as any person over 5'10" instantly discovers.

Some other owner, however, poured a fine slab and erected a big barn-like building behind the house, lined with sturdy shelving. It had been used as a shop, and even had a huge metal structure to hoist engines from vehicles. It's the reason I bought the property, because the shop is now a big well-insulated studio space, where I can slop paint

Thyme • Surprisingly pretty flowers, excellent in the rock garden.

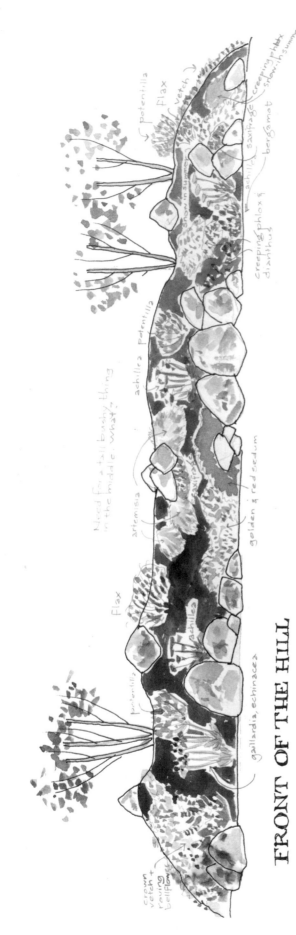

FRONT OF THE HILL

Potential hill plants
——————
a mix of creeping & clumps of taller.

Creeping: Dragon's blood sedum (Gurney's) ✓
    Crown vetch   " ✓
    Golden Sedum   " ✓
    Nancy's roving bellflower   " ✓
    Creeping phlox   Gurney's ✗

✓   Snow-in-summer   Nursery(?)
✓   Dianthus   " ✓
—   Candytuft   "
—   Saxifrage   "
✓   Artemisia   "

Gurney's
——————
  Vetch: 20 plants   14.00   ⟨30 for 17.49⟩
  Red Sedum: 10 plants   14.00   ⟨15 for 17.29⟩
  Golden Sedum: 10 plants   14.00   ⟨15 for 17.29⟩
  Phlox: 8 plants   13.25

          66.00

Taller: clump or two gaillardia & echinacea ✓
    two or three potentilla ✓
    some achillea ✓
    a bergamot ✓
    Flax !

  3 artemisia   15.00
  3 potentilla   30.00
  2 saxifrage   10.00
  3 echinacea   15.00
  3 snow in summer 15.00
  5 dianthus   25.00
  1 bergamot   5.00
  bark chips   30.00
      145.00

Flax, gaillardia : sharon
achillea : Hannah seedlings
roving bellflower : Nancy

$211.00 — whew!

1. The house
2. Potting shed
3. Terazzo
4. Terazzo bed
Yarrow • Foxglove • Saxifrage Gaillardia • Lemon Balm Nicotiana fragrans • Blue Flax • White fireweed • Purple coneflower • Pansies • Pinks • Potentilla • Rose campion • Lambs ears • Petunias • Cranesbill geranium (Johnson's blue) • Poppies • Blue Lace flower • Scabiosa •
5. Bark chips
6. Big spruce
7. Old yellow roses
8. Rock garden
Golden Sedum • Dragons blood sedum • Sedum kamschata Mother of thyme • Crown Vetch • Creeping Phlox • Snow in summer • Basket of gold • Salvia blue hill • Rover bellflower • Fringe sage • Monarda • Lilacs Silver mound artemisia Poppies • Yarrow • Catnip Cat mint • Veronica • Canterbury bells •
9. Wildflower bed
Mix: first year lots of annuals and scarlet flax. Second year biceffies & native grasses.
10. Seedling bed
Started from seed this year under lights. Lavatera • Annual larkspur • Lettuce Spiked salvia • Heliotrope • Bronze fennel • Four o'clock Coral nymph salvia • Nicotiana silt • Sunflower varieties
11. Big perennials
Bearded iris (4 varieties) • Small larkspur • Tall delphinium • Centaurea Montana • Hollyhocks
12. Island Bed
Trolleus Europeanus • Spike Veronica • Gaillardia •

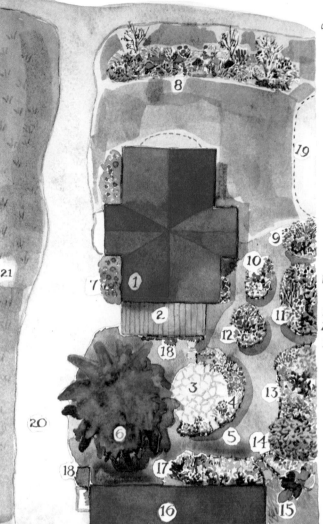

anemone • Double buttercup • Foxglove • Saxifrage
13. Original bed
Poppies • Hollyhocks • Columbine • Painted daisies Miniature iris • Siberian iris • Sorrel • Thyme Lavender • Burnet • Mint Speedwell • Chives • Penstemon • Mallow
14. Old lilac
15. Rhubarb
Weedy cat hideout • Compost
16. Barn/studio
17. Studio bed
unusual sunflowers • Cleona Cosmos • Asiatic lilies • Maltese cross • Feverfew • Canterbury bells • Centaurea • Blue Flax • Yarrow • Cat mint • pansies • petunias • Scabiosa
18. Hop-vines
Twining over potting shed and studio doorways
19. Next year's beds
20. Driveway
21. Weeds
This garden was created from scratch in three years. Only things present were the rose hedge, the ancient lilac and the spruce tree. Many of the original plants came from gardening friends, many were started from seed and the rest came from local nurseries and garden catalogues. Want to trade?

around and throw papers on the floor and indulge in any kind of creative frolic.

When I moved in, the yard itself was denuded of vegetation, employed as a dog run for years. Only one beleaguered lilac bush remained, a hedge of senescent yellow roses, and a big impervious spruce. So I was able, first sketching and giving shape to my visions in the journal, to create a tiny oasis from the wasteland, made of perennial beds edged with woven willow fences, broken up by bark-chip trails.

Though this is only a small lot, it came with a weed-choked "back forty" (about 20' x 70'), out behind the barn. The principal weed, a vicious thorny vine that looks like it might be a member of the nightshade family, sends shoots through the foundation and into the studio. Until last fall its tangles hid old car parts and inscrutable pieces of steel. I removed as many as I could find, but knew the place could never be transformed without some agent more capable than I. So I built a fence and a rickety little shed, and fulfilled the eleven-year-old's dream of having a horse in her backyard. In this case, two boisterous colts, who have been more thorough than any herbicide in removing every trace of vegetation back there, and who are still pawing up angle iron and galvanized pipe. When they go to spring pastures, I'll till the newly fertile mess under and saturate it with wildflower seeds and buffalo grass.

In the adventure of restoring the house to some of its original dignity, and in the obsessive delight of planning and planting gardens, and then in exulting over all the gratifying changes, the journal has moved into a new phase. It's reflected in the lists of flowers, the careful notes about seed ger-

mination and seedlings, the designs for rock gardens, the sketches from little corners of the house, with comfortable cats. I've never had the chance to work my full aesthetic will on a house or a piece of ground before, and it absorbs nearly all my attention. I've entered a more active, less reflective period. For now, the self can take care of itself; I'm more interested in seedling-searching than soul-searching.

Each clean empty page spread is still an emblem of the wellspring of being, the inexhaustible source for me. The journal has come steadily through all the changes despite many pages filled with tirades of self-loathing, the torment of the young person bewildered by her first encounter with depression, or breathy portraits of the latest beau's perfections. Pages of tying of the self into

knots, making simple things complicated and complicated things impossible. And then later, all the attempts at cleverness and sophistication, the affected world-weary tone, the smug accounts of conquests and triumphs, shoring up a shaky self-image.

It's painful to revisit those pages, they look like so much ineffective wheel-spinning now, even though the joys of the world still emerge in them. Volume 24: "I have to just give up being distressed at my lack of distress over leaving Jacques for Wyoming. I saw early the signs that said don't stop here too long. How far did I see or go into his life? He's vulnerable but he does that by choice. I pretend to be vulnerable but no one really gets inside me, and probably never will. Last day in the woods, paddling around like a riverboat on a raft in Jacques' pond, slowly drifting to several inches of shore, letting newts rest on my hands, picking out bodies of dragonfly larvae clinging to the rushes, finding two frogs hunkered into the sphagnum moss."

Looking at that shelf full of books, I can imagine that every grimace and sob was necessary in this slow crafting of a life. And for the most part the journal, with its soul-searching and patient rumination, has acted as the great bringer of order, again and again. Even in the bleakest of times, the mere act of writing has allowed me step outside the bleakness, in the act of capturing it. It has been the field of resolutions and the renewal of vows. I can reach back through the pages to that girl with the May wreath on her head, and test what she said back then about the newness of the world, find out if it is still true. I can speak to her, and most certainly listen to her, since she was anything but quiet about the great joy she had discovered. In fact, I can ensure that what she said *is* true, by continuing

Dusk by the river. Spotted sandpiper calling alarm notes on the gravel bar. Water dropped again after the 2" deluge, exposing the elegant shorelines.

Very still, cool & damp. Admiring the sharp tips of the spruces.

to affirm it, first in the journal, and then with that foundation, in life.

This book is meant to be a distillation of what years of journal-keeping have taught me. I've tried to describe some of the ways, intentional and otherwise, that it captures vivid cross-sections of a life, and also show the kind of transformations that take place on the page, back to life, and onto the page again, over the course of many volumes. The act of recording a life, in healthy solitude and active connection to loved terrain, is also the act of creating a life.

I see the effect of journal-keeping in reverse when I don't do it for a while, for whatever reason. I begin to feel a kind of malaise, an indigestion of the spirit; too many experiences have accumulated, without being truly seen or felt. The journal has become a necessary extension of my thinking, feeling self. If nothing goes into it, I become slightly disconnected, unresponsive, less than alert. The solution for that is usually an entry of thousands of words that leaves my hand paralyzed and my spirit blissfully spent.

If our lives are vessels, continually being filled, then each of us needs a way to empty them. That emptying can take dangerous and destructive or creative forms; an explosion of energy or an outpouring of love. The journal is a place to decant the stuff of life; reassuringly, none of it is wasted. It remains fresh, still tasting of its source. Transferring experience from the vat of life into the vessel of the journal is a distillation: it sieves, concentrates, and ferments. If after many seasons we develop some mastery of the process, the stuff can become as clear and fiery as brandy.

Elk trail to the clearing
Hannah Hinchman

Start with a smell, like a crushed marigold leaf, burning leaves, the sea, coal smoke, melting asphalt, swimming pool chlorine, mown grass. Try to transcribe the pictures that form themselves in your mind's eye under its influence. When the pictures are secure, try to bring associations into mind-view: atmospheres, moods, times of day.

Cast your memory back to a time when you became aware of yourself in the world, but not the world of judging elders or jeering peers. Write about a time when you really noticed what season it was, and why you noticed it. Try to recall an incident when you were alone, outside, and awake.

The last couple of decades have taught us to think of our childhoods largely as something to recover from, whether we are afflicted with low self-esteem, memories of abuse, or other troubles. As a result, most of us have assembled a cache of story-memories that sum up or "explain" our early years; many of them amount to a kind of revisionist history, taking on the spin and the interpretation of the times. Such scrutiny is valid, but it leaves out too much. I'm suggesting a series of written entries, revisiting childhood and adolescence, that will form a different portrait: the you that lived on the ground under the sky.

Can you remember a time, as a child or a youth, when you were either enchanted by being outdoors, or terrified? Tell the story. Ask yourself when you felt most at home, when the universe of grass and trees, woods and creeks, gardens and fields, streets and parks seemed to belong to you. How did you respond to it, what did you do?

Write about an encounter with an animal, either wild or domesticated, that stands out in memory. We commonly truncate and embalm real memories by turning them into stories told the same way each time: "that was when the roost-

Up the hitching rack drive Here is a beetle hurrying to cross. When I touch him with my boot he up-ends as though trying to stick his head in the sand.

this fellow a casualty too — fell intact out of the sky

Memory Walking at the
HOUSE ON TREMONT RD.

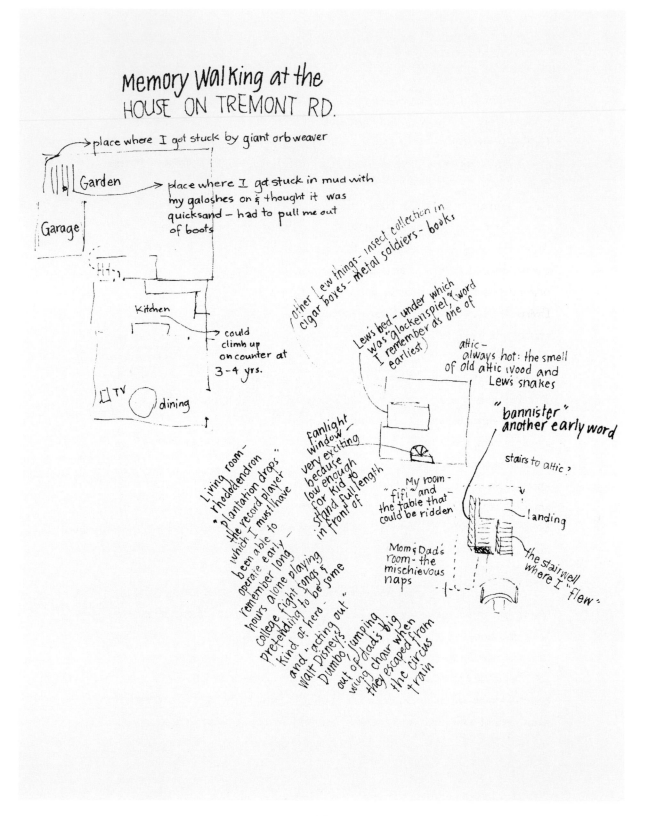

→ place where I got stuck by giant orb weaver

Garden

→ place where I got stuck in mud with my galoshes on & thought it was quicksand – had to pull me out of boots

Garage

Kitchen

→ could climb up on counter at 3-4 yrs.

TV ○ dining

Other I ew things – insect collection in cigar boxes – metal soldiers – books

Lew's bed – under which was "glockenspiel," word I remember as one of earliest

attic – always hot: the smell of old attic wood and Lew's snakes

"bannister" another early word

stairs to attic ?

landing

the stairwell where I "flew"

My room – "fifi" and the table that could be ridden

Mom & Dad's room – the mischievous naps

fanlight window – very exciting because low enough for kid to stand full length in front of

Living room – "rhododendron" "plantation drops" the record player which I must have been able to operate early – remember long hours alone playing college fight songs & pretending to be some kind of hero – and "acting out" Walt Disney's Dumbo jumping out of dad's big wing chair when they escaped from the circus train

18

er chased me." As the story becomes more ritualized in the telling, actual sensations are forgotten. Revisit the experience with your original eyes and search for forgotten details.

In the most oppressed life there are sanctuaries and refuges. I would guess that even the truly desperate have experienced with relief, however brief, a quiet moment in an empty lot, with the sky overhead, and maybe a crescent moon.

Where did you escape to, growing up? A refuge can be something as large as Aullwood, or as tiny as a circle of flattened grass in a field. It can be a hole in the hedge or the top of a tree, or an empty playing field. When did you first begin to see this place as a refuge? What did you do there? Everyone has at least a handful of memories that aren't set in rooms. If they are collected, they form a bridge, a continuum between that person and the one who lives now, who either continues to seek out that elemental relationship with earth and sky, wishes he had time to, or has forgotten how.

If you live in a place that includes a yard, make a diagram of it, and describe what kind of a place it is, or imagine it from an aerial perspective. What goes on there? Is it an active or a contemplative place? Perhaps it's an ignored place: if you don't go there, why? Is there anything that would make it more habitable? Make a diagram-sketch of some changes you'd like to make there, no matter how fanciful. In your sketch, transform it into the refuge you've always wanted.

If you don't have a garden, but have a space for one, no matter how tiny, plan it and sketch it. Then dig it up and do it. Observe it carefully, and document what happens there all through a growing season, from the time the plants begin to emerge until they have died.

If you are already a gardener, use your journal to get to know your plants better, and experiment, visually, with changes you might make. What if that wall were covered with clematis? What if that forlorn patch of lawn became an island

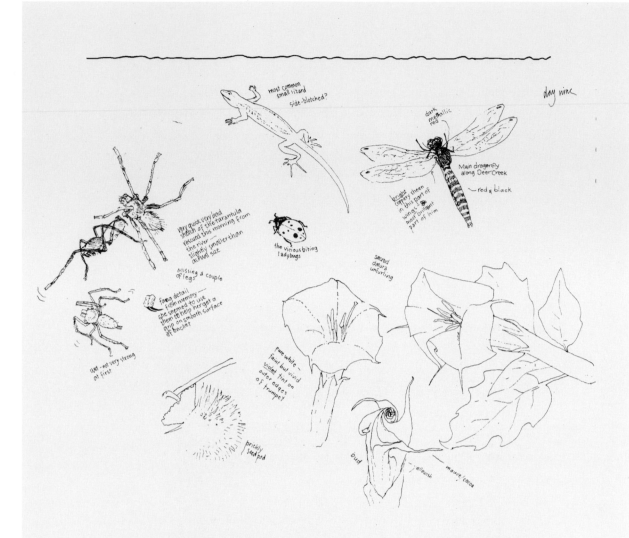

bed? Select a couple of the plants you find yourself admiring every day, and get up close to them. Examine the structure of the plant, and draw it. Then do a sketch of its overall look, just an impression of it. How does a columbine bud form, and where are the long spurs hidden before it blooms? What does an iris blossom really look like? How best to capture the feel of a peony?

If you are lucky enough to have a big piece of land, or a farm, get to know it thoroughly, go beyond the vocabulary of landscaping, gardening, or crops. Learn its nature and its secrets. Wander across it without a goal, the way you wandered as a child.

If you are beginning a first journal, christen it with an exhaustive written entry, hours worth of writing, following whatever thought-thread draws you. Only one caveat: each time you find that the writing is beginning to wrap itself up in analysis, or judging, or creating arguments for or against, stop and immediately turn to something concrete and tangible. Then let that lead you where it may.

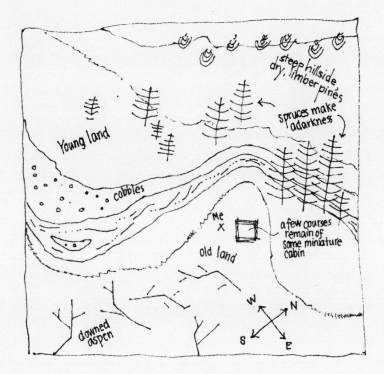

22 October
Still frosty in my hillside hideout.
Can't get enough of these
elaborately curled leaves, their
bending planes, and want
some kind of curling lettering
to match.
But need to use the thick part of the brush too.

Nearly finished with
Beth Merrick's
Oxbow painting which has a selection of curly leaves in it.

The big storm is on the way; I see its advanced farmers

Chapter 2

WET, DRY, ROUGH, POLISHED

Children know all about the mystery of drawing. Drawing (in fact, all the arts) should be taught right along with language, emphasizing equally its mystery and utility. Art is considered expendable, even suspect, these days; yet our media-atmosphere is more and more saturated with images. It would be wise, since the visual is used to manipulate us, for us to learn early on how to manipulate the visual. A nation full of competent little artists might be more intoxicated by, but less susceptible to, the power of the image.

Remember the slick paper, sprayed with water, and the smell of the viscous finger paints dolloped onto it? It's a powerful memory for me, because it is attached to the primitive thrill of creation, perhaps the first time I came under its spell. Long before the urge is born to translate mental pictures into tangible form, the desire to play with "stuff" is in our fingertips.

In the ancestral environment, that must have been of enormous value, since our antecedents made every necessity, every tool and every adornment by hand, from raw materials. Someone with a sense of rhythm could learn to winnow well, some patient soul who enjoyed feeling the kernels of maize break down in the stone trough would grind the best meal. Certain water pot makers would understand the heft and the strength of the clay better than others, and be able to make the lightest and the strongest vessels. But they didn't stop there, either: they added beauty to utility so consistently that we have to consider the yen to embellish as something fundamental to our nature.

Frustration, though, is born right along with the thrill of shaping. The marks and smears we make with the finger paints soon lose their novelty. We push the colorful stuff around, but the shapes we make don't match our internal vision, in brilliance, complexity, or magic.

And right from the beginning, teachers confuse

CONTÉ AQUA PENCILS

FEB 23

us by praising our drawings no matter how far short of our vision they fall. The message is: nothing is really expected of this. One is as good as another. There's no encouragement to excel, to master skills that would bring deep satisfaction. As Betty Edwards says in her ground-breaking book *Drawing on the Right Side of the Brain*, we treat visual skills as if they were rare and mysterious, granted only to a few. But we expect everyone to master the basic skills of language.

Part of the problem is simply the materials we provide: they are limited, of poor quality, and performance is never really demanded of them. In my grade-school era, the first colors children got hold of, after finger paints, were wax crayons. We were instructed to choose a color, stick with it, and make a neat, even layer that stayed inside the lines of George Washington's hat or the turkey's tail. We struggled to master that skill, producing pale, drab exercises that had nothing to do with the lurking thrill hovering around the box of crayons itself,

Let's see here...this feels so damn scratchy. Trying different nibs. This one seems less given to snags...handles color well. I'll try it, but practice some more first.... With this nib a thick/thin thing can occur

with its prismatic array of pure colors. Now, most children have sets of big bright markers that don't blend very well, and they use them on absorbent newsprint or construction paper. No wonder they feel disappointed! It would be like trying to learn piano on an out-of-tune instrument, with some of the keys missing.

Since there are obviously ways of learning to draw, why not pass them on to everyone? Why wait until the most gifted and persistent sort themselves out, and encourage only them, leaving everyone else in a more confined world? It would be easy enough for a teacher to say to a child who is obviously disappointed with his effort, "What were you seeing? How big was the horse compared to the girl? Why doesn't the horse look right to you?" Then send him back to the desk with the right tools, and the clues that can help him hone his vision. The teacher doesn't need to be a Degas for that, just as a teacher of language doesn't have to be a Tolstoy.

Everyone should learn to draw competently, with a sense of play and invention, if only to honor the fact that it's one of the first instinctive gestures we make to appease the appetite for beau-

ty. If everyone acknowledged that hunger, and gained a whole selection of ways to satisfy it, a different culture would emerge.

As a child, there were times when no available drawing tool could touch what I was after in the way of extravagant beauty. Only glitter would satisfy the craving. I went through a glitter and jewel phase that my mother, amazingly, indulged, taking me to the hobby and craft store whenever we went to the shopping center. I'd come home with bags of plastic rubies and emeralds, and the little tool that allows you to affix gems to clothing in a tiny stud of pronged metal. I'd cover sheets of sequins, and best of all, hover over great vats of glitter that winked in the dim aisles of the store. I would stare into the depths of the blue and think that nothing could be so exquisite, only to turn to the red, and be swallowed up in its radiation of redness, like the scene of the ruby slippers in *The Wizard of Oz.*

Many of the gems found their way to inappropriate spots, especially after I learned about Elmer's glue. My mother wasn't as happy as I'd hoped she'd be when I decorated her favorite martini glass with a row of enormous stones, all

1.

13

14

13

16.

17.

18

19

20.

21.

22.

23.

24.

	13
1	
2	14
3	15
4	16
5	17
6	18
7	19
8	20
9	21
10	22
11	23
12	24

1. Graphite Gray
2. Lunar Black
3. Payne's Gray
4. Raw umber
5. Burnt Umber
6. Permanent Brown
7. Quinacridone Gold
8. Green Gold
9. Olive Green
10. Sap Green
11. Terre Verte
12. Prussian Green

13. Yellow Ochre
14. Indian Yellow / Cadmium Yellow
15. Winsor Yellow
16. New Gamboge
17. Alizarin Crimson
18. Cadmium Red
19. Deep Scarlet
20. Quinacridone Rose
21. Indigo Blue
22. Carbazole Violet
23. French Ultram.
24. Cerulean Blue

CAN TRAVEL

Plan for afternoon in badlands
Photos for later, careful use
Notes to extract from or beef up
Small, on-site watercolor sketches

materials
Journal for notes?
Small watercolor sheets
Small w/c set/ brushes
Brush pen
dip pen?
Permanent markers
Non permanent markers

Arrival of water — that it moves
amoeba-like, hesitant, stopping
and starting

around the rim. The climax of one summer's informal neighborhood ballet production (I had choreographed it, and also designed the costumes: sequins from start to finish) was for the assembled dancers to shower the dazzled audience with hand-fuls of multi-hued glitter. I'm sure I could find some in the yard around Brenda's patio if I looked tomorrow.

Now I've come to appreciate colors that go beyond the primary, and glitter is not the only thing that seduces me. In nature, alongside the standard sky-water-flower loveliness, we find a whole world of mixed, odd, changing, undefinable colors. I'm thinking now of a group of beginning watercolor students sitting with me on a hillside in Yellowstone Park not long ago, and of the palpable dismay in the air as they looked down at the

dozen lumps of paint in their boxes, and back at the thousand and one colors in the real world in front of them.

I asked them to make a quick simple pencil drawing, so that they would have an underlying form before taking up the brush. So: a wide flat valley, the winding Lamar River, a timbered slope overlapping a more distant slope—simple shapes for our purposes. The sun below the horizon, but still plenty of rich summer light over everything. I wanted them to get the feel of mixing paint: how much water with how much pigment; a loaded brush or a dry brush; a pale wash or a saturated color. Then we'd work on building up complicated colors with transparent layers. Before I could deflect them, though, they'd begun making puddles of paint that led straight to grade-school lockstep.

With Science School class at Dornan's

Trees are green. Water is blue. Grass is green. A green on the palette looks like it's supposed to be grass, and a darker one looks like it should fit for pine trees. This was a group of intelligent, capable adults, but the paint and the brushes "thumped them back into the bassinet," as poet Louise Bogan put it in one of her letters.

In this case, the meadow included a range of colors from olive-bronze to sand dun. The river, against shadowed banks, reflected a lemony peach from one quadrant of the sky. When it made a turn and appeared against the meadow, it carried a patch of steely blue like the highlight on a magpie's tail. The evergreens weren't green at all, but a violet-umber. The distant hill was related in color to the violet of the evergreens, but softened by an atmospheric blue wash.

One of the women had begun to be overtaken by disgust and disappointment, stabbing her brush around heedlessly. I decided that it would be better to start all over again, to get everyone to slow down, get close to their colors and their brushes and their paper, find out first what these materials could do, what they *wanted* to do, before joining them to images.

So for a while we simply mixed colors. We painted small squares on the paper, and watched the way they dried. We layered other colors on top of the wet and dry squares. We paid attention to what happened when the brush carried a heavy load of paint and water, ready to flow and pool when it touched the paper, and the very different results when the brush carried only a light load. We tried mixes of opposite colors to get greyed tones: a little violet touched into a pool of chrome yellow, a hint of sap green in alizarin crimson.

In fact, we never turned back to "landscape" painting that evening. It got dark while we were still completely absorbed in trying to mix a color to match the cliffs lit up by the last of the light. And everyone was satisfied. There was a certain inaudible hum in the air, as in a hive of contented bees, among this group lost in conversation with the simple, noble tools of art.

Over the years I've come to regard the tools I use as friends, some finicky and balky, some joyous and ever-ready, but each with its own manner and signature. And that doesn't mean that I've become more snobbish about them, insisting only on Kolinsky-tail brushes. In fact, I've just rediscovered medium-size ballpoint pens, your basic Bic. Whenever I write with one, I start to make round-

EMMA VISITS WATERING CAN

ed, balanced, soft letters, nice and big. I can't help it, the pen tells me what to do. Even taking down phone messages on the little legal notepad beside the answering machine can be a comforting, sensuous experience using that simple ballpoint on the mattress of the pad.

I like the Bic much better than the heavy, pretentious Mont Blanc ballpoint pen that my friend found in the street, in a little pouch with a matching pencil and fountain pen, and gave to me. It's unbalanced, and the tip is stingy and stiff. But the

Nettie is
half-listening . . .

Mont Blanc *fountain* pen—there is a truly lovable tool. When I write with it, my text is bold, clean, stylish, dashing. Yet each pen changes when I use it to draw—the Bic is relaxed but unambitious, the Mont Blanc fountain pen is too conservative to make really passionate marks.

The way I handle my art tools is akin to the way I pet my cats. Oreo has a dense pelt, with lots of guard hairs, so I tend to plump him like a pillow, to hear the hollow sound. Emma is flinchy, so I pet her delicately in isolated spots, never stroking her all the way down the back and out along her tail. Ratz doesn't care how you handle him, he loves any of it, but will throw his head back ecstatically and flatten his ears if you scratch him under the chin. Sally arranges her own petting configuration, rising to meet your hand and applying different parts of her body to it, including her cold nose. Flax is sleek and satiny, loves the kind of sinuous stroking that Emma hates—except when it's cold. Then he resents having the fluffed-up air space in his coat flattened, because it's his insulation.

There are certain things I like to feel when I pet my cats, and there are certain things *they* like to feel when I pet them, so we reach an agreeable middle ground. A similar arrangement exists with my pens, pencils, brushes, paints, and papers. There are certain touches that suit them, that they

respond well to. And there are certain things I want to feel when I'm using them. In my little pen-jar are a half-dozen similar looking metal dip-pens. The one with the red holder is for use only on smooth paper or illustration board, because of its well-broken-in precision. I looked at it once under a 30-power hand lens and discovered that through long use, its left flange had been polished down to fit exactly the angle at which it meets the paper when I hold it. Another of the pens is peculiarly flexible, and I like to use it for a copperplate-style script, because it produces the proper thick and thin lines with special fluidity.

Among the watercolor brushes are old favorites, some so battered as to look useless to brush snobs, but I know them so well that I can predict what they will do, no small virtue. I was given some new, very fine brushes, and am just in the beginning stages of getting to know them. The smallest new brush, a 3x0, has been a disappointment because it has the worst of tendencies: to divide into two separate clumps, instead of staying pointed.

As you are inspecting brushes, unobtrusively lick them and see if they will hold a good point. I know it sounds unsanitary, but I'm willing to take a chance in order to come away with a properly made brush. Among the tiny brushes, buying the most expensive is no guarantee of getting one that's well-behaved. In the bigger sizes, you usually get what you pay for. But even if you feel confident about the one you've bought, it will take a long time to learn its nuances, its gifts, and what you can trust it to do.

I love to watch students learn about pencils. Most of us think that pencils come in two varieties: sharp and dull. But for a few bucks you can buy a set of six drawing pencils, with varying degrees of hardness. A 6H, for instance, will produce a smooth, pearly gray surface. Even if you press as hard as you can, you will never achieve anything darker than a medium gray. At the other end of the scale, your 6B (for black, I assume), will make a grainy gray, darker and rougher even in its lightest application than the 6H. And if you press hard, you can create an area of rich, satiny graphite black. In between lies a whole range of grays, more than you ever thought possible. And textures as well: the hard pencils leave a smooth trail of graphite, the soft ones tend to bump along the surface of the paper leaving visible minute traces of the white page.

Most of us think that a sharp pencil is what emerges from a pencil sharpener. How can that be, when only a stubby cone of lead appears at the tip? With an Exacto knife, you can carve away the wood to expose a long length of lead, then shave it down towards true sharpness. Finally, you can sand it on a piece of fine sandpaper to create a long, delicate point that stays sharp for quite a while. A sharp point isn't always required: for smooth areas of gray, it helps to develop a flat facet on the lead while you are working, to help you get an even tone instead of a series of discrete strokes. (If you do a lot of pencil drawings in the journal, purchase a

can of spray fixative, otherwise the drawings will smear beyond recognition).

As examples for my students, I always hand out reproductions of conte crayon drawings by Georges Seurat. You'll find at least one in every comprehensive book on the history of drawing. Conte crayon acts like a soft pencil, but since it's made with carbon instead of graphite, the black is truer, without graphite's gloss. Seurat used a rough

paper, like charcoal paper, so that he could control the light or dark tones by contrasting a light touch, which let the paper texture show through, with a heavy one, which blotted it out. He created absolutely readable images without employing a single line. Up close, the drawings just look like areas of tone, a few different grays, an area of pure white left open. But at a little distance they resolve into luminous, clear pictures, all managed solely by shifts in tonality. The same effect can be achieved in the journal with a heavyweight (6B) or charcoal pencil.

Another of the ahhh-moments of drawing revelation comes when students see that they can capture dazzling sensations of light and shadow with just a few pencils. But to get there requires learning a new vocabulary of tones. Just as we can sense the difference among air temperatures, we can learn that we have more choices than just black, white, and gray.

I'm still on a restless search for the perfect journal. It needs to be filled with good paper, heavy and smooth enough to resist bleeding and bleed-through. Ideally, the paper will be something other than bright blue-white, because to my eyes colors look better on a gentler background. I'd consider a toned paper, since it's fun to add highlights with white colored pencil or gouache (opaque water color), but not too dark to Xerox (I like to send journal pages as letters sometimes, and I also use the artwork as illustrations, as in this book).

The book needs to be bound solidly enough to open flat without breaking, and once it gets broken in, to stay open to the desired page, as well-thumbed dictionaries do. I think that requires a sewn binding, though there may be sophisticated new technologies out there. Spiral bindings,

So many varieties of roundness — but I've chosen a rockscape where light is being swallowed by shadow

though they offer flatness and the ability to be folded back on themselves, have two disadvantages: the spiral creates a break in the page spread, no matter how small it is, and you can't write the number of the volume on the spine. I am constantly searching through past volumes for quotes, events, garden notes, etc., and it would be maddening to have to take every book off the shelf to check it. And I cherish a bit of old-world feeling about this, too: I want these several shelves of books to be authentic, handsome volumes, not high-school notebooks. I don't care what the cover looks like, as long as it's tough enough to withstand the interior of knapsacks and to be laid out on rocks. A touch of waterproofing on the cover would be nice.

For volumes 52 and 53, I've selected the kind of blank book with a white canvas cover that the manufacturers urge you to decorate. I have, in a big way, with acrylics and glued-on bits of watercolors (no glitter yet). The paper these books contain is serviceable, and there are enough pages in them to carry me through about a year. I prefer a long book, so that I can accumulate a body of time, making it easier to review the way life is unfolding. But the paper in these volumes is too white; it has neither refinement nor personality.

My friend brought back from Lucca, Italy, a couple of exquisite blank books. They are the finest I've seen, with all the features I crave (except cover waterproofing)—the paper itself is enough to make you weep—but each one has only enough pages to cover a couple of months. I'm reluctant to make a commitment to what I know will be only a short-term affair.

All this material-gossip has one real goal behind it: to get me to pay attention. To get closer, to slow down, to use a loving, inquiring touch. I can't think of any work of integrity in which the materials aren't respected, known intimately, and asked to perform at a high level. That's part of what moves us when we admire a piece of art, though we may not recognize it. This is all part of not staying on the surface of things, but of dwelling, really dwelling, in the moment that contains all the sensations. In the best drawings and paintings you can isolate any section, any square inch, and find evidence that the artist attended carefully to it. That it wasn't a mechanical act, that he was present when he touched it.

My essential tool kit:

- The journal

- A clip or clips to hold the pages in place. Wind-ruffled pages are annoying and hard on the eyes.

- Three pencils, hard, medium and soft

- A little slice from one of the big white plastic erasers that erase cleanly and without abrading the paper

- Exacto knife and sandpaper

- A handful of fiber-tipped pens, both water soluble and waterproof, like Pilot Razor Points and Pigma Micron pens. The latter are waterproof, with tips in a range of sizes. They aren't as satisfyingly precise as drafting pens like rapidographs, but they are far less temperamental.

- A little traveling brush, in case I want to dip it into my water bottle and touch it to the lines of a drawing made with the Razor Point, to make a beautiful blue-gray wash.

- A double-tipped Sakura Pigma Sumi Brush. The tips are just as pointed and flexible as a regular brush, one large, one small, but they are made of bendable, permeable felt-like material, with their own ink supply. For quick gestural brush drawings, and to lay down large areas of black, they are indispensable, and much less complicated than carrying jars of ink into the field. To extend their range of possibility, leave the cap off one for a couple of hours and then it will produce a soft-edged grey tone rather than its usual aggressive black.

Back in the studio I have all kinds of equipment to add to the basics, but the following are never far from my grasp:

- Two fountain pens; the Mont Blanc and a Rotring "Art Pen," the sketch version, with an extra-fine nib. The little ink cartridges that fit the Art Pen also fit the Mont Blanc. I use both of these almost exclusively for text rather than drawing.

• A selection of calligraphy nibs in various widths. Of all the brands I have tried, Mitchell Roundhand is my favorite.

• A variety of drawing pen nibs, from the most delicate size, a crow quill, on up. These require dipping, so I keep different inks, including waterproof India, on hand to use with these, and also a few bottles of liquid acrylic ink. They were an experiment, but I'm so pleased by their brilliance that I use them in both dip and calligraphy pens. This brand, FW, is reputed to be lightfast, a failing in brilliant inks of the past. (Both calligraphy and dip pens, as well as many other calligraphy supplies are available from a mail-order company called Pendragon. You can get a catalog by calling 800-775-PENS)

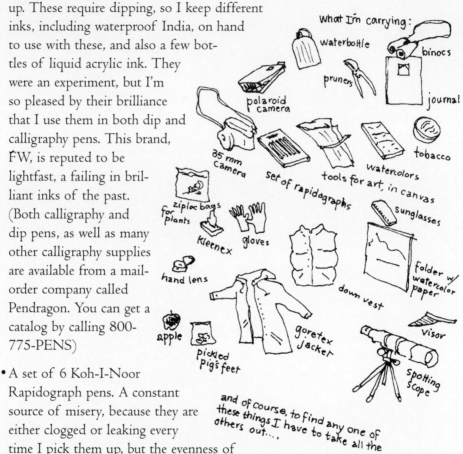

What I'm carrying:
waterbottle
binocs
pruners
journal
polaroid camera
tobacco
35 mm camera
watercolors
set of rapidographs
tools for art, in canvas
ziploc bags for plants
sunglasses
Kleenex
gloves
hand lens
down vest
folder w/ watercolor paper
apple
goretex jacket
visor
pickled pig's feet
spotting scope

and of course, to find any one of these things I have to take all the others out....

• A set of 6 Koh-I-Noor Rapidograph pens. A constant source of misery, because they are either clogged or leaking every time I pick them up, but the evenness of the line is unbeatable. At the moment I'm trying out a new pen made by Grumbacher, an aerodynamically delicious thing called the Artist Pen. Its line is exactly the same quality as the rapidograph, and looks as though it can't possibly leak. However, I'm wary of its disposability. I won't buy another one unless the ink supply lasts a long, long time. I couldn't comfortably buy a whole pen for $4.75 and then throw it away a month later. Some of my students appear in class with something called a Ceramicron, another throw-away rapidograph substitute, but I've never been able to locate one.

- A compact watercolor palette that has spaces for 24 colors. There isn't much room for mixing, but it fits easily on my drawing table, ready to provide color for the journal or other small pieces. For more ambitious works I get out my big plastic palette; it also holds 24 colors, but more of each, and provides space to mix up quantities of color, required for large areas of wash.

- My watercolors themselves are a collection from Winsor Newton and Daniel Smith, in tubes. (Daniel Smith is an extensive art supply house in Seattle, whose catalog is my lifeline. Call 800-426-6740 to get one). Daniel Smith has just introduced his own line of watercolors, and I'm very pleased with them, especially some of the unique new colors like green gold, lunar earth, and undersea green. Because most of what I paint is in nature, I'm always searching for unusual organic hues to extend my basic palette. Many brands of watercolors are weak in those areas: the greens especially bear no relation to any color I've seen in nature. No matter how cleverly I mix, they still have a synthetic look to me. Winsor Newton and Daniel Smith have the most sympathetic array of colors I know, and the paint quality is exquisite: lots of good pigment, highly transparent.

- Another useful water-based paint is known as gouache (pronounced 'goo-wash'). Unlike standard watercolors, it is opaque, so each layer can cover the one beneath it. Mixed to the consistency of ink, it makes the ideal medium for color calligraphy as well. Though purists would never combine it with watercolor, I'll admit that it's saved a number of doomed paintings for me. When I've been too liberal with dark values, it has allowed me to restore some light to the image, though that's considered cheating in watercolor circles. I use Winsor Newton gouache.

- I have combined two sets of colored pencils: 120 Prismacolors and 72 Derwent Artist's Pencils. They are arranged by hue and value. Just looking at them provokes a frisson of desire in me, and using them is just as good. When I finished sharpening them all for the first time, I made an enormous list, 10 feet long, with squares of each color applied dark to light, next to its name. I don't really *need* so many pencils, because layering them produces new colors so readily. But I love to be absolutely specific about a color, especially in the early stages of a drawing, and this chromatic lexicon helps me make fine distinctions and also suggests new possibilities.

- A bottle of liquid mask, sometimes called frisket. It's latex in a watery form, and can be used with pens, brushes, or other tools. When you apply it to paper, it forms an impermeable rubber film that can be painted over once it's dry. Later, the frisket rolls off like rubber cement, revealing either brilliant white paper, or an earlier color that you wanted to preserve. (Be sure to swish your brush around in water instantly and thoroughly after applying it, though, and don't use your best brushes—if the mask dries in the brush, it's nearly impossible to remove).

Even though none of the journals I've ever worked with contains paper that stands up to heavy watercolor applications (the paper buckles or saturates), I continue to use it sparingly anyway, usually in small areas, and in a less watery mixture. If you want to try all kinds of paper without buying big, expensive sheets of each one, order paper sample packets. Both the companies mentioned above will send you an impressive array of samples, about 4" x 4", each one identified, for between $7 and $12.

When you approach a new medium for the first time, do as my Yellowstone students did, and spend a lot of time experimenting before you launch into a drawing or painting. There are so many variables, even with something as basic as a pen. Each paper surface produces a different effect. You may use a simple line, or build many lines up into a tone, or achieve a tone with clusters of dots. The ink may be waterproof, or break up into shades of gray when water touches it. Each tool will have a different feel. As with dance partners, it takes a while to adapt yourself to each style, and still longer to achieve effortless grace.

There are warehouses of instructional books out there that will try to show you, step-by-step, how to reproduce what another artist has done. If you use them, you will add to your skill, but possibly injure your own vision. Books that explain basic techniques, but don't try to dictate your method, are the most useful, I've found. Here are three that I have near me all the time: *Nature Drawing, a Tool for Learning* and *Field Sketching*, both by Clare Walker Leslie, and the *Encyclopedia of Watercolor Techniques*, by Hazel Harrison.

Don't let the materials intimidate you. Err on the side of boldness, in pushing them to their limits and beyond. You can always go back to restraint and subtlety. But be willing to *wallow* in the colors, shapes, and surfaces, for as long as your exuberance sustains you.

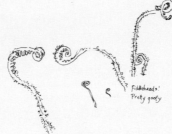

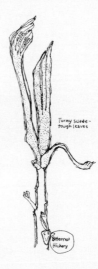

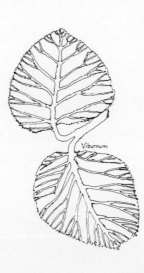

dozing standing up

face towards sun

dozes & chews cud

finally really sleeps

Chapter 3

FEELING IT IN YOUR BONES

When I was a little girl I ran everywhere, jumping hedges and gardens on the way. Walking seemed prosaic, "pedestrian" and inefficient, when running and leaping got you there faster and allowed you to revel in strength and grace at the same time. It's better to say that I cantered instead of ran, since my body at the time was not a person's but a horse's, and moved in horsely ways. As a horse I could jump over things that people couldn't, easily clearing four-foot fences that made even the bigger boys in the neighborhood quail. The identification was as complete as imagination would allow, to the point of tethering the horse outside school to wait for my return.

Nearly all my friends, especially women, report a similar phase of centaurhood before puberty forced us into sadly human bodies that in some sense are no longer our own. I miss that world; it was exhilaration itself to feel my legs as the powerful, long-striding legs of the Black Stallion, and to stay in perfect balance, with a light touch on the reins, over impossible obstacles. I still feel the joy, not so much of athletic prowess, but of "fitness" —moving over a rough landscape without stumbling, boulder-hopping confidently, and climbing and descending efficiently, putting the stress on large muscles instead of joints. And I feel it while dancing, reaching light-footed transcendence in a good western waltz, or even in rhythm with the urban techno-pop of aerobics class. But it's not quite the same as "becoming" a horse.

Fitness has become an obsession in the last two decades, spawning a "no pain, no gain" subculture. These are the people who run, bike, and ski with a grim and joyless ferocity; they believe the endorphins flow only if you court injury or collapse. I'm confused by this, recalling moments of most perfect athletic achievement as being marked by a sensation of ease and effortlessness, even in the midst of great exertion.

GERANIUMS LOOK PRETTY....

BUT LOSE ALL THEIR PETALS IF YOU BREATHE ON 'EM

I'm unwilling to let go of that ideal; it lies at the heart of how we move through the world. A state of "flow" appears, or disappears, according to the pleasure we find in using, or even simply inhabiting, our bodies. A person need not be a fatless machine striving to better a personal best, in order to move and live with grace and deftness.

I no longer run everywhere I go. Some of that physical energy has been diverted into the effort to shape images and words that mean something and carry a measure of vivacity. But the love of, and the ability to craft language, colors, lines, is permeated by the same physical delight. Sometimes the pen on the page is alive, and sometimes it seems stupid and stumbling. Often I wait, bending over that dark pool full of hidden words, and suddenly the right ones surface. I'm ready for them, and feel something of the same keen pleasure as I did when speed and strength became equipoise over a jump.

Other times the pool stays blank, just a maddening lifeless flatness. The presence or absence of flow can't be dictated, but a person can remain agile and alert, ready to recognize and act on whatever comes.

The pleasure of encountering the next blank page-spread in the journal seems never to diminish, and it's also grounded in the physical. There is that provocative emptiness again, with its edges that don't have to be edges, and a shape-shifting ability to go from two to three dimensions, and back again. There is the yielding surface of a good

SALVIA 'BLUE HILL'

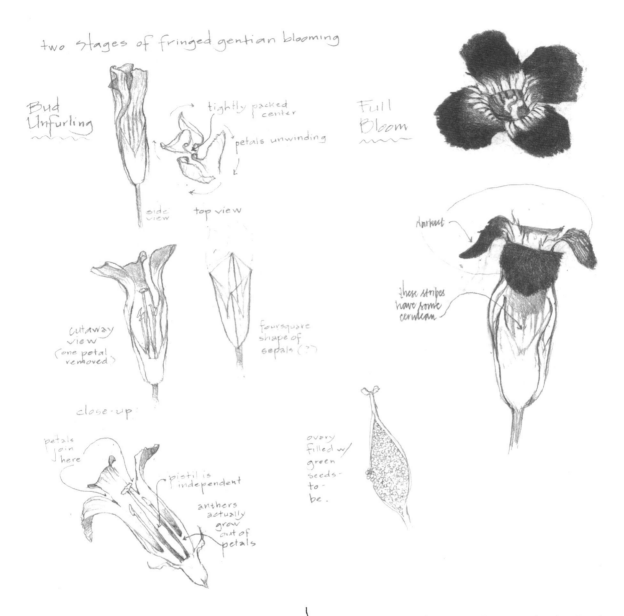

two stages of fringed gentian blooming

Bud
Unfurling

tightly packed center

petals unwinding

Full
Bloom

side view

top view

cutaway view
(one petal removed)

Foursquare shape of sepals (?)

darkest

these stripes have some cerulean

close-up:

petals join here

pistil is independent

anthers actually grow out of petals

ovary filled w/ green seeds-to-be.

paper, waiting to reveal new ways of layering colors.

I may fling down a sketch in a moment, if my cat happens to be doing something droll, and then the page has received the seed of its structure. Or it may begin with a deliberate and soothing geometry: blocks of intricate text building up like rows of knitting, a tension between organic form and implied vertical/horizontal axes. The book, the pages, are physical things, and the way I make something with the raw materials is handiwork.

There is nothing like the feel of the tip of a reliable, familiar pen gliding over the paper, leaving a crisp trail, and the sense of control in the fingers shaping beautiful letters. Especially early in the morning, before a cup of coffee has rippled the stillness of the waking state, to write is to luxuri-ate, and fulfills some indescribable need. Then there is the boldness of brush lettering, the coop-eration between the tip of the brush, which has its own shape and tendencies, and the guiding hand —working out a plant-like pattern made of thick and thin, curved and straight, sharp and rounded marks.

It took many years of writing, thousands of pages, to discover that I could not find the fit between experience and record by writing with "summing up" words. To say that a canoe trip was wonderful, and that the river was beautiful, and that I had many adventures accomplished nothing in the journal: I didn't even have the pleasure of reliving the best moments while writing about them. And yet this ingrained tendency to general-ize I still have to fight daily. A journal filled with "nices," "wonderfuls," "terribles," and "interest-ings" is one drained of any live juice. If that kind

of writing merely reflects habit, there is hope for change. If the writer insists on it, consider it a sign of a deep-seated fear of the real.

The act of writing regularly tends to solve that problem on its own, though. In such narrow con-fines we bore ourselves, and don't bother re-reading passages because we know they won't recall the flavor of the moment. After a while, we begin groping for something more, the magical formula that will make experience live on the page.

The best way to avoid the trap of dead words is to keep a firm grip on the real stuff, prickly, slimy, or bony as it may be. The vitality of the body and the senses can get smothered by the language we encounter daily. Think how we are awash in gutless speech: the space-filling of the report, the obfus-cation of the academic paper, the evasion of the political statement.

As an antidote, pick up the journals and poetry of Gerard Manley Hopkins, or Colette's memoirs,

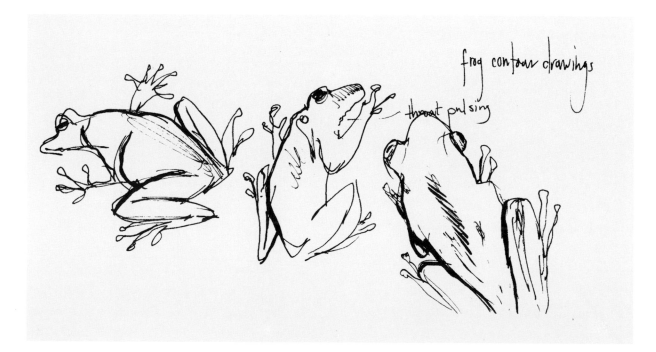

frog contour drawings

throat pulsing

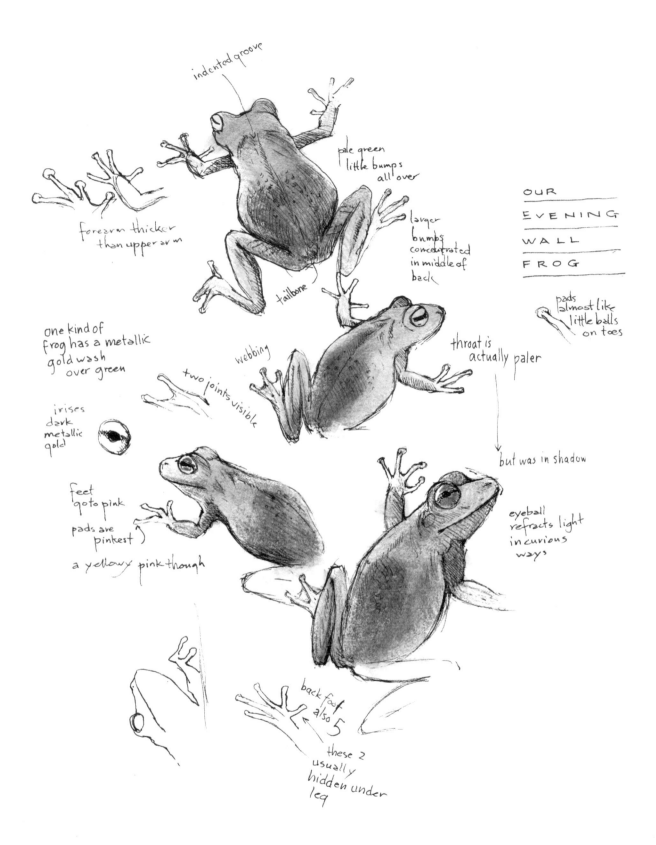

indented groove

forearm thicker
than upper arm

pale green
little bumps
all over

larger
bumps
concentrated
in middle of
back

tailbone

OUR
EVENING
WALL
FROG

pads
almost like
little balls
on toes

one kind of
frog has a metallic
gold wash
over green

webbing

two joints visible

throat is
actually paler

irises
dark
metallic
gold

feet
go to pink

pads are
pinkest

a yellowy pink though

but was in shadow

eyeball
refracts light
in curious
ways

back foot
also 5

these 2
usually
hidden under
leg

47

NATIVE WOODLAND
Botanical Garden. Chicago

and see how language can come directly from the senses and the intelligence of the body. Here's what Hopkins says in his journal of something so ordinary as observing pigeons: "They look like little gay juds by shape when they walk, strutting and jod-jodding with their heads. The two young ones are all white and the pins of the folded wings, quill pleated over quill, are like crisp and shapely cuttleshells found on the shore. The others are dull thundercolour, or black-grape-colour, except in the white pieings, the quills and tail, and in the shot of the neck. I saw one up on the eaves of the roof: as it moved its head a crush of satin green came and went, a wet or soft flaming of the light."

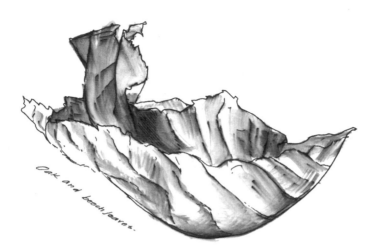

Oak and beech leaves.

It's good practice to write at such a delirious sensory pitch from time to time, just to spice up a diet of dry latinates: all those —isms, —ologys, and —ations that serve a useful purpose but haven't much flavor. Keep alert for dense, rich words, and don't hesitate to fling them around. How about "fox," "dirt," "leather," "squirt," "chafe," "warp," "vortex," and "crinkle"? Being on good terms with words like that will keep you from losing yourself in the labyrinth of the abstract and the over-intellectual. I'll never be able to cross a mountain torrent, now, without thinking of Hopkins' "crispest endive sprayings."

And cleave to verbs. A drifting, off-target account can suddenly ignite if you insert the right verb. There are plenty of verb-gems languishing out there that deserve to be polished up and placed in new settings: dissolve, mirror, badger, uproot, winnow, slather, suspend, carve, blot, bundle, contort, revolve, flood, crumble, dither, tamp, utter.

With drawing, the taproot into the body is inescapable, no matter how many "artists" have tried to pry it out, for whatever pathetic reasons. The marks on the paper don't just stand for something, they are the thing itself. Overlay them with rhetoric as you will, these are marks made with earthly substances on a wide array of surfaces, by someone's hand.

With words and with some forms of painting, you have a chance to rework and revise, cover your tracks, so to speak. With a drawing, the whole history of what you saw and what you did about it is revealed, or can be revealed, unless your aim is a Charles Scheeler-like seamless perfection. As a record of inquiry, there is nothing to compare to a drawing. Each drawing starts with nothing, and reinvents from the ground up. I'd much rather look at a messy page of sketches by Rembrandt, as he goes over and over the lines, pushing and pulling forms, splashing down a hasty wash for a shadow, than I would contemplate his most finished portrait.

There is no denying the allure of illusion, and most of us at one stage or another have marveled

at the artists who are able to make things look "real" (or nowadays, like a photograph). To create the illusion of three dimensions on the page, to capture light and distance and atmosphere, fur and stone and feathers by manipulating color and contrast is one of the highest artistic skills. But those who arrive at that mastery have had to pass the world through their skins for years, give themselves over to visceral empathy for a long apprenticeship, before they produce what we call finished works. And because I honor that long dedication, so hard to define and justify, I would rather look at the works that show not only the hand of the artist plainly, but the choices, instincts, and revisions that went into their making. Rembrandt feels the sag of the thatched roof as he draws it with his flexible quill pen, he doesn't translate it first into words and ideas, then construct a formula. Gustav Klimt follows the spare hollow of a woman's ribcage, and finds a similar arch in her jaw, tracing it with the most sensitive of pale pencil edgings. These are not planned, or plotted or even thought, they are just the body's intuitive dance with the things it loves.

It's no surprise that every artist I most admire —Degas, Bonnard, Rembrandt, Pisarro, Da Vinci, Toulouse-Lautrec, Morris Graves—drew and painted animals. It almost seems to be a law of nature, that if you revel in the senses, are comfortable with appetites, feel understanding, empathy, and admiration for the body, then you must have animals around you, to look at or to touch or both. At this moment I'm lucky enough to live in a place I can share with cats (five) and horses (two), while reaping the fellowship of my neighbors' six goats and their big dog. If it were possible, and someday I hope it will be, I'll live a life like Tasha Tudor, author and illustrator of children's books, whose Vermont farm teems with geese, goats, corgis, pullets, and parrots. I'll add snakes, spiders, toads, wasps, birds, mice, and whatever else happens along.

Nothing returns us to a sense of well-being and steadiness like a dog ready for a walk, or a cat rolling in the warm dirt of the garden. I actively participate in the one's joy and the other's giddy comfort. I can hear the thud of the colts' hooves as they mock-battle each other in the corral behind the studio. To find the place on my cat's neck that he loves most to be scratched, or the spot under the

delphinium pods

jaw that makes the colt close his eyes in bliss, is itself a bliss, irreducible.

To draw these creatures is another way of loving them and knowing them. Only once in every dozen drawings do I get something that has a bit of cat-nature, even though I'm closer to them than to any of the other animals. As a horse-child I spent hundreds of hours trying to draw horses, all from step-by-step handbooks which left me with no real skills or insight, but only an ability to copy a narrow set of coordinates. Now, when I draw my horses from life, I

FIELD
GUIDE
TO INSECTS VISITING RABBITBRUSH
between 11:00 & 11:30 a.m.   *on Friday, August 30, Blacktail Ponds*

actual size

very small bee
with black & white
abdomen which he curls
tightly around clump of
blooms

large tachinid fly —
nervous. Black & white,
very shiny thorax

Classic black &
yellow bumble
bee.

Empty insect
eggs — neat hole
drilled in ends.

Many leaves like this —
in each of them, under here
is a small spider in a
small sheet web.

Handsome brown "argyle sock"
caterpillar eats cherry leaf,
then tries to curl up &
hide in brown part

nearly always fail. The sketch ossifies into the same old set of gestures, and the spirit is lost.

By now, I've gained a basic understanding of the anatomy of the horse, and think about the structure beneath the skin and muscles as I'm drawing. That's the only charm that seems to break the curse of childish habits. It will be another several decades before I will learn the curve of the neck, or how to convey the springi-

ness of the pasterns, but I have plenty of time and lots of blank pages for that.

The similarities and differences among the skeletons of four-footed mammals demonstrate a wonderful economy. Many different forms are achieved simply by extending or compressing different bone passages, without major rearranging or reconstruction. And if you imagine in fast motion our transition from four-footed to upright crea-

color of mushed grubs

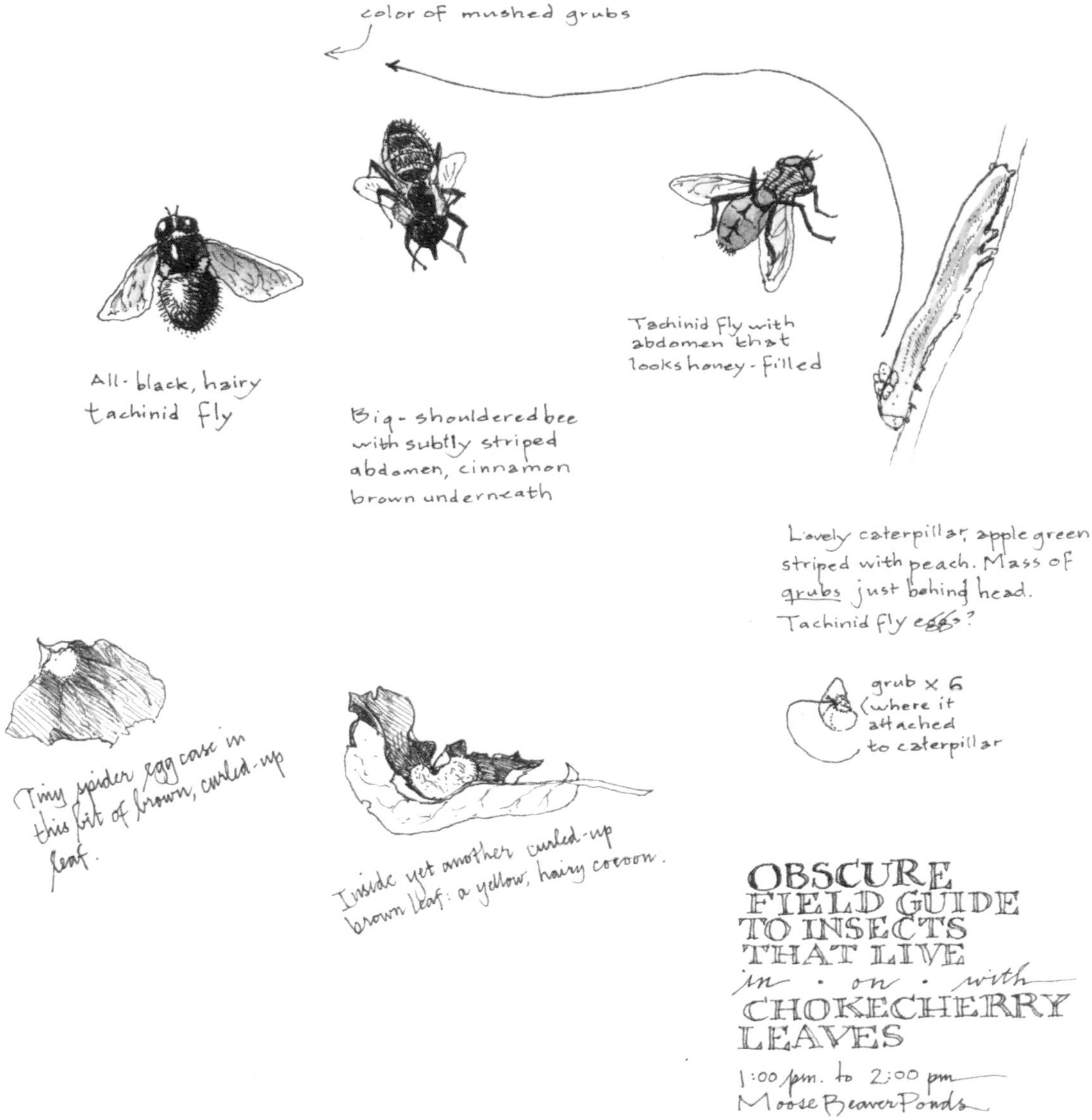

All-black, hairy tachinid fly

Big-shouldered bee with subtly striped abdomen, cinnamon brown underneath

Tachinid fly with abdomen that looks honey-filled

Lovely caterpillar, apple green striped with peach. Mass of grubs just behind head. Tachinid fly eggs?

grub × 6 (where it attached to caterpillar)

Tiny spider egg case in this bit of brown, curled-up leaf.

Inside yet another curled-up brown leaf: a yellow, hairy cocoon.

OBSCURE FIELD GUIDE TO INSECTS THAT LIVE in · on · with CHOKECHERRY LEAVES
1:00 p.m. to 2:00 pm
Moose Beaver Ponds

tures, you can understand how the same basic set of bones has settled into different configurations, and why our knees and spines are still so subject to troubles. (A horse's knees don't bear anything like the same weight-load.) As I draw my cats, the horses, the goats, or even the bison in Yellowstone, I tend to hunch and stretch, bend joints, instinctively feeling their gestures inside my own bones and muscles. Feel what happens to your hand when you try to draw the wing of a bat!

This kind of body-empathy can extend beyond other animals. I've just turned back to this chapter after drawing the seedpods of a larkspur from my garden. When I was really paying attention, I could feel the brittleness, the attenuation of the twigs inside my limbs and hands like another skeleton, and the infolded, stretched roundness of the seed vessels like the stretched roundness of my own

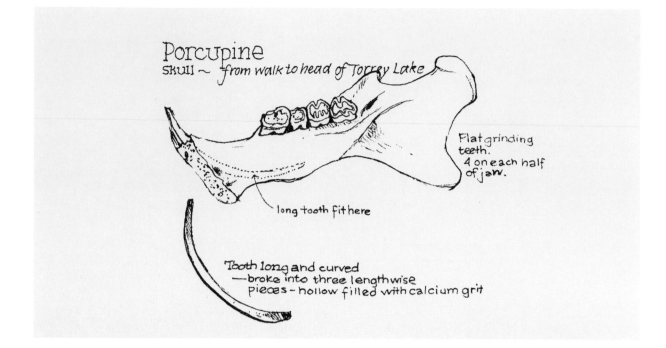

Porcupine
SKULL ~ from walk to head of Torrey Lake

Flat grinding teeth. 4 on each half of jaw.

long tooth fit here

Tooth long and curved —broke into three lengthwise pieces ~ hollow filled with calcium grit

cheeks when I eat two cherry tomatoes at once. For convention's sake we usually talk about "seeing" and "observation," but it would be more accurate to talk about feeling or identifying with the forms. The act of drawing is an absorbing tactile enchantment: you feel the shapes inside your body, and your body wields the tools that capture the shapes.

Working on a portrait of a friend, I watch as that most elusive of effects, a likeness, begins to form, dissolves, then is brought back into being again. The visceral and the analytic both come into play in the course of the drawing. The visceral comes first, as I try to intuit an expression, feeling the weight of the brow or the thrust of a chin. Analysis doesn't work at this stage, because a likeness is more than just the sum of the features, and must be grasped as a whole. When something has appeared on the page that begins to approximate a likeness, then I can analyze and compare, emphasize

or tone down, but that's also when the physical act of making the right mark becomes a high-wire act.

The ability we have to "recognize" someone, even at a distance, suggests that we all have an unexamined, not to say hidden, vocabulary of the physical. Body language influences us, patterns of expression, tone of voice: an array of cues allows us not only to recognize, but to read the meaning of an action. We're only now beginning to investigate scientifically how this "gestalt" way of knowing operates in the brain, but there's no doubt it's an ancient acquisition.

In the pages of the journal, this ability to grasp "wholenesses" can be cultivated, we can get better at reading the body language of the world. The overall expression of a season, the measure of stress, or of health and vibrancy in a landscape, a garden, a cat, the psychic atmosphere of a city street, the meaning of the robin distress calls in the back yard, the subtext of a friend's conversation: all are understood viscerally. The attentive journal keeper will try to find the means of bringing those undercurrents to the page, and will have to be inventive to do so.

When the horse-girl realized that there was no turning back from the inexorable march into womanhood, she extracted several promises from the woman-to-be: that she should always be able to do an aerial cartwheel, that she should never hesitate to sit on the ground, and that she should continue to try to learn to pick up spiders. I've made good on two of them. Sitting on the ground—in fact, making a point of getting my face close to whatever is going on in nature, whether it requires wading, lying stretched out, or clinging to a cliff face —is one of the best ways I have of keeping the horse-girl alive. Three years ago, I was able to pick up a very large orb-weaving spider, heavy as a square of baking chocolate, when I accidentally knocked it from its web, and since then I've made great strides in spider handling. And I can still do a terrestrial cartwheel, which serves the purpose almost as well as an aerial one.

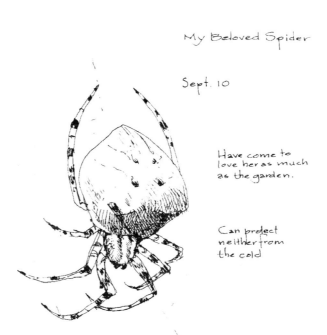

My Beloved Spider

Sept. 10

Have come to love her as much as the garden.

Can protect neither from the cold

Use the journal to interview your body. Which muscles are underused, and which are hardy and durable? Have you reduced your way of walking to the most utilitarian pace, or do you have a variety of strides and degrees of buoyancy? How do you tend to stand and sit? What are your hands like? Are they curious grubby hands or aristocratic cared-for hands? Do you feel confident walking on a log over a stream? Swimming in big ocean waves? Scrambling down a steep hill? Are you at your best on the tennis court, or with a spade in your hands, or on the dance floor? Do you feel yourself to be flexible, or have your muscles and ligaments settled into a narrow range of motion?

Writing about this may be cause for justified pleasure that your body is a happy, expressive creature. Or it may make you feel miserable, because you know that you fall far short of being as fit as you wish you were. But if you find yourself with little to say, because you have lost touch with your body to such a degree that you just can't answer the questions, it might be a good idea to reacquaint yourself with "Brother Ass," as St. Francis referred to his body. Simply walking, starting on easy flat ground and working up to hills and rough country, is a splendid way to do that. We all know how to walk, more or less (and if you think about it, walking itself is a pretty complex physical act), but we can try to add polish to the basic stride, emphasizing grace, strength, or springiness.

Use the journal to document not only your increasing knowledge of and

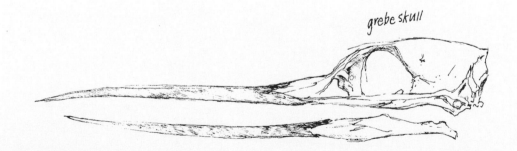

grebe skull

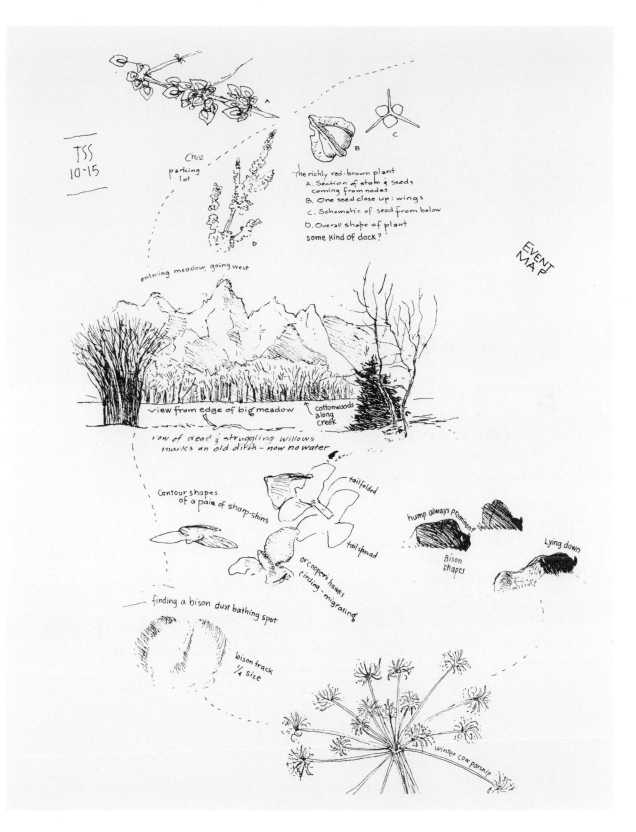

TSS
10-15

Cross
parking
lot

A

B

C

The richly red-brown plant
A. Section of stem & seeds
   coming from nodes
B. One seed close up: wings
C. Schematic of seed from below
D. Overall shape of plant
some kind of dock?

D

EVENT
MAP

entering meadow, going west

view from edge of big meadow

cottonwoods
along
creek

row of dead & struggling willows
marks an old ditch — now no water

tailfolded

Contour shapes
of a pair of sharp-shins

hump always prominent

Lying down

tail spread

Bison
shapes

or coopers hawks
circling - migrating

finding a bison dust bathing spot

bison track
¼ size

winter cow parsnip

57

pleasure in your body, but of what catches your eye while you are sauntering around. Here's a way to escape from the linear "first I went here and saw this; then I went there and saw that" narrative. When you return from your walk, use a page or a generous space in the journal to write down word-images of things you noticed, scattering them over the space. As more recollections come to you, you can append details to the basic collection of written images, making clusters

OCT 13

NOTE: THE TERRIBLE WEATHER THAT WAS SUPPOSED TO COME DID NOT.

OCTOBER 14
hike with the hill neighbors to near nymph lake then barbara & I walked back in glacier basin through swathes of gold grass - "tussocks", "hummocks" dark plaits of marsh. stream ponded by beaver dams along the way. Two mallards. Odd conversations, she is so beautiful, accentuates my dumpiness she loves deer, looks like one. If she's a deer what am I?

A MARMO T.

wandering around naming peaks watching the last watercolors in the sky started gathering little dry grasses & flowers that I could barely see. Something about the delicacy of their structures must have stood out in the near darkness.

of observations. The whole assortment is likely to be made up of sentence fragments and phrases, and you may discover that the words you use in them are more vivid and pointed than the ones you would have chosen for a conventional account. In this way, you create an authentic "skeleton" of your journey, which is then fleshed out and bound together by your wealth of recollection.

With a picture of a human skeleton in front of you (or a real skeleton if you can find one), fill a page with fanciful and speculative sketches about how the same bones could be transmuted into dog, cat, horse, bird, gerbil. Stretch and shrink bones, fuse or separate them, bulk them up or pare them down, flatten or elongate them. If this intrigues you, find out how close you came in your redesigns by looking up pictures of animal skeletons. . . or better yet, visit your nearest natural history museum, where they are sure to have a number of mounted skeletons on display. What is happening to the skeleton inside the body of a sea lion or a seal? Does a snake have hips?

Draw your pets. To avoid the terror of trying to get a proper-looking ani-

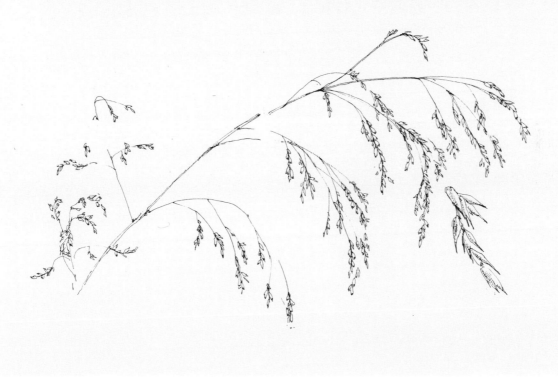

mal down on the page in its entirety right away, work up to it by studying different parts of their bodies. The muzzle of a cat. Your dog's paws. The various ways your cat bends or extends its front paw while grooming it. Your parakeet's feet. How a dog's back leg is constructed. Breaking the form down into these more abstract shapes will allow you to look at them clearly, and sidestep your urge to make a dog-symbol or a cat-symbol. You probably don't have a ready-made symbol for a dog's leg, which means that you'll have to look at it with blessedly unclouded eyes.

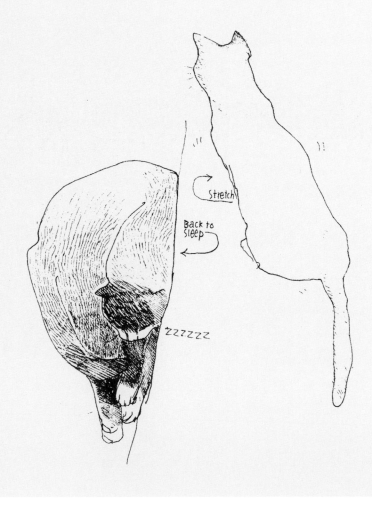

Initially, it may help to simplify the drawings into geometric shapes: curves, ovals, squares—but don't get stuck on the geometry. Keep remembering that an eye is a spherical object encased, protected, and positioned by the bones of the head—it's more than a two-dimensional shape. Be willing to feel the bones in your bones.

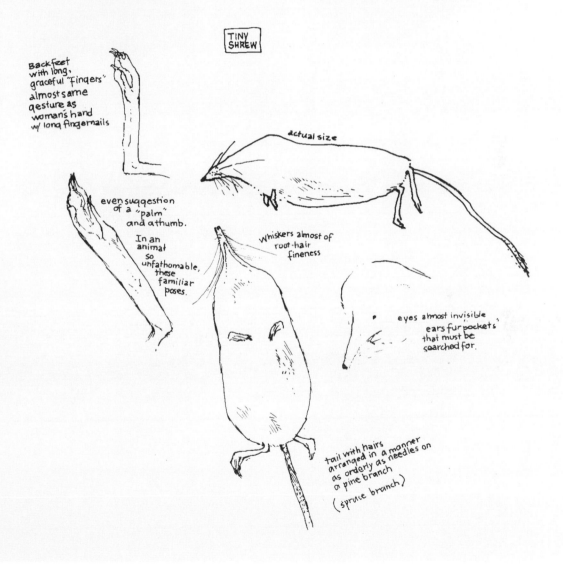

TINY SHREW

Back feet with long, graceful "fingers" almost same gesture as woman's hand w/ long fingernails

even suggestion of a "palm" and a thumb.

In an animal so unfathomable, these familiar poses.

actual size

Whiskers almost of root-hair fineness

eyes almost invisible

ears fur pockets that must be searched for.

tail with hairs arranged in a manner as orderly as needles on a pine branch

(spruce branch)

Johson's Blue Geranium

Oriental Poppy

Yarrow

Fringe Sage

Catmint

Centaurea Montana

Snow on the Mountain

Chapter 4

THE POWER OF THE ORDINARY

Last March I found in the basement an old fluorescent light fixture left over from renovation. It set me reading in earnest about how to start flower seedlings indoors, and pretty soon I had cobbled together a 3' x 3' plastic-tented nursery in the living room, with the light fixture set on the lowest rungs of two ladder-back chairs, and a variety of kitten-exclusion devices around the bottom. In four big flats I planted seeds of foxglove, yarrow, gazania, poppies, veronica, forget-me-not, campanula, and lemon balm, and hovered over them almost hour by hour.

During a trip to Bozeman, Montana, around the same time, I visited a garden center I'd heard about, and came away with a dozen gallon containers of well-established perennials, representing my grocery money for the next two weeks. I had momentarily forgotten that Bozeman, though 200 miles north, sits several thousand feet lower, which makes an enormous difference in the progress of spring. I settled the perennials on the floor in front of the sliding glass door, in among the geraniums, assuming that they'd find places in my garden in a couple of weeks.

But not only had I ignored what I knew to be true about spring in Wyoming, this turned out to be the wettest spring on record, and most of the precipitation came in the form of snow. In late April it was still snowing, the seedlings bursting out of their starter pots, the perennials languishing from pot-binding and overwatering. Some of them died in the house, and the others—all but two—died when I planted them outdoors prematurely. In mid-May the seedlings had to go in the ground, and for another several weeks the garden looked like a landfill, with buckets, plastic sheets, plastic bottles, and cardboard boxes strewn over it in an attempt to protect the babies from the snow

Birds RETURNING

February 23 · Junco
February 25 · Kingfisher (not sure he ever really left)
March 20 · Robins
Late March · Flickers
          Great blue herons
          Bluebirds
          Killdeers
          Song Sparrows
          Redtails
          Kestrels Swallows
April 22   Ruby crowned kinglets
          Cassin's finches
          Snipes
At skyline pond, late April:
          Buffleheads
          Mergansers
          All teal
          Black necked stilts
          osprey (nesting)
          Eared grebe
          Shoveler

May 8 - White crowned
          sparrows
          Audubon's warblers
May 13   House wren
          Frogs croaking
May 14   Black-headed grosbeak
May 15   Broad tailed hummer
          Western tanager
          Sapsucker
          Calliope hummer
June 1 - Yellow warbler
          Warbling vireo
          Western wood pewee
          Y.B. Sapsucker
June 3 - Nighthawk
June 17 - Swainson's thrush

and cold, all hastily removed whenever a ray of sun broke through. It didn't stop snowing until June tenth, then overnight it was midsummer.

Most of the garden survived, especially the plants that had come from wise Wyoming plants-people, but none of my seedlings ever flowered that summer. My impression of that spring is as a dark, dim, cold, and wet time. I kept digging through snowdrifts to look at the base of the columbines and the blue flax, which were pushing out shoots anyway. I did a lot of hand-wringing, and cursing myself for my folly, and shuddering when I felt the wind shift around to the east again, which around here means a good week of rain or snow. The early returning birds suffered, too,

mountain bluebirds and robins hunched under evergreens and hedges, the only pieces of bare ground in sight.

And yet, rereading the account of that time in the journal, I find another story. Two stories really: one wild and one domesticated, but both having to do with the tenaciousness of the spirit, and its determination to please itself. I diverted my attention from the gloomy garden prospect by watching for subtle indications of the inexorable move toward spring. On May first I wrote: "Still snowy, sodden, bitter. All the time, though, treefuls of red-winged and yellow-headed blackbirds setting up such a clamor that I think the poor elderly woman, who I saw this morning pushing a

FIELD
GUIDE
TO
Things

Snow
Does

1. Snow melts faster where something dark sits on it.

2. Snow sticks to itself and builds up on small surfaces

3. Snow will bend, sliding slowly over the edge of a roof, showing the prints of the roof

4. Where the whole pile of snow on the roof is exposed at the break point, you can see that each snowfall made a layer and the layers stay distinct

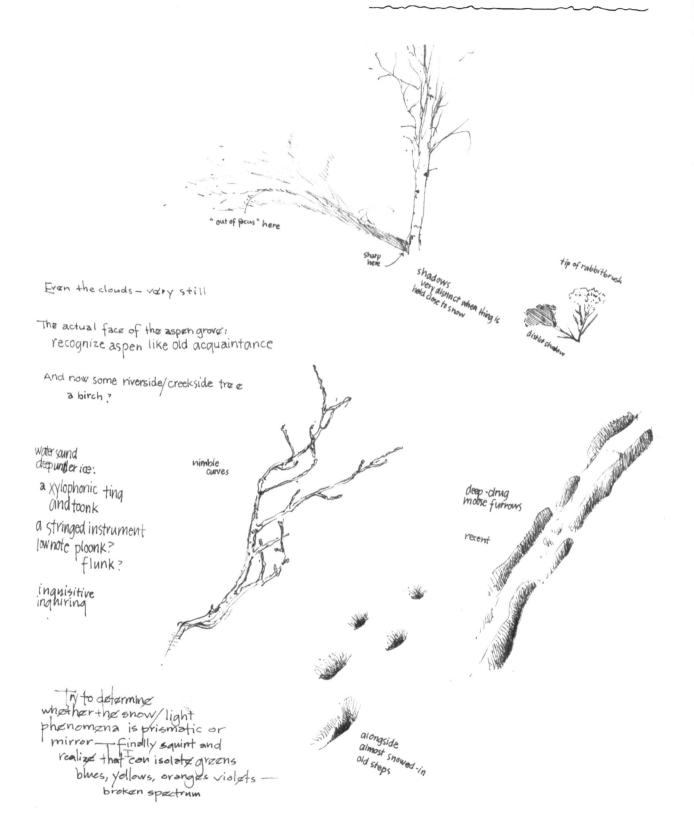

"out of focus" here

sharp here

shadows very distinct when thing is held close to snow

tip of rabbitbrush

distint shadow

Even the clouds — very still

The actual face of the aspen grove:
   recognize aspen like old acquaintance

And now some riverside/creekside tree
   a birch?

nimble curves

Water sound deep under ice:

a xylophonic ting and toonk

a stringed instrument low note ploonk?
      flunk?

inquisitive inquiring

deep-drug moose furrows

recent

alongside almost snowed-in old steps

Try to determine whether the snow/light phenomena is prismatic or mirror — finally squint and realize that I can isolate greens blues, yellows, oranges violets — broken spectrum

That dry lichen that seems to be independent of the ground

wheelbarrow-load of logs to her cabin, must be going mad with the noise (she lives under the bird trees). A tree full of redwings is tolerable—a medley of their watery first notes mixed with the ending trills is raucous but musical. Insert the yellow-heads, though, and you're deep in cacophony. 'Oink-oinkle-BRAAAAACK' (raspberry) is what they sound like next to 'Conk-kler-REEEE' of redwings. Huge herds of them collected here when they should be distributed on territories and into nesting." There was a peculiar pleasure, tinged with defiance, in going beyond the sodden drabness and finding something funny and interesting about those birds. I'd never tried to write down what the yellow-headed blackbirds sound like before, but I laughed as I did it, and that caused a little shift in the faultline of gloom.

The list of returning birds grew longer, though it continued to snow. Out in the sagebrush, the hardiest of little plants opened leaf rosettes flattened against the ground, and the dense cushions of vetch extended tentative folded-page leaves, furry as young mice. I discovered how much swallows depend on insect hatches over ponds during rough spring weather. I strolled on the glacial moraines, and appreciated again the strange-but-beautiful hues of lichen on the big boulders—celadon, neon orange, black, yellow, gray, and white—which are at their best when wet, and in somber light conditions. I made a collection of lichen-covered rocks of a size I could lift, and set out the basis of a rock garden, already dreamed and designed in the journal. Along the creeks the willow wands had colored up, bright wine and bronze. I cut armloads of willow branches, both stakes and withes, and wove a willow edging for the flower beds.

At home during the many solitary days in the studio and the house (a wet spring seems to dry up small-town social life), the journal tells me that I set apart many domestic moments, and lit them up by simply describing them: "Here we all are quiet on a snowy late afternoon-evening in April. There's Flax in his attitude of total relaxation, propped against the back of the couch—he was propped against me until I moved. Oreo and Emma Dilemma are quietly thrashing around in the bowl of the Papasan chair (now wholly devoted to cats). They sleep entwined, then wake and groom each other until, typically, a fight like this breaks out. Never lasts long. I want to stay put in this room, at the moment with all five of my companions snoozing around me. Windless and gray outside,

snow falling as it never did in winter. Not a soul on the streets. So here is a classic situation of spring in Wyoming: you get to understand the nature of snow so much better than you do in winter, because you have 12 hours of daylight to study it in, instead of 8."

Or, on April 25th: "Cats & I pent up all day. Snow started tapering off after all the chores done (Laundry! Now I've resumed my polar-fleece pelt —it's all I ever wear—but at least it's clean for the moment). After a glass of wine, at 7:00, we all

seem to want to go outside, since the wind has stopped and it's still about 36 degrees. Emma's up on the potting shed shelf & I start throwing tiny snowballs to her (this is real snowball snow). Amazingly, she either bats or catches each one. I get more enthusiastic. 'Come on all you animals, let's build a snow fort!' At first they don't understand what I'm doing, rolling up snowballs, but as soon as the snowballs become a wall that I hide behind, they *do* get it. I lob snowballs, Emma fields them, outdoing herself with impossible flinging leaps to catch them. Pretty soon they move in for the final assault. I've poked a spy hole in the wall, and paws come through it, as well as over the top. I get a glimpse of Emma through the hole with that quivering, dilated-pupil look— next instant she's burst through the wall, snow flying everywhere."

What started as an effort to fill a few idle moments while dinner was cooking turned into an impromptu celebration, though outwardly there was little to celebrate. Inside again, I quickly drew a series of memory drawings of the snow fort, and for some reason the drawings picked up the zaniness of the occasion. They are some of my all-time favorite drawings. So far, I haven't been able to achieve that "style" again.

A long-running journal is an invaluable document, because it records something other than the time-and-goal-dominated anxiety that drives us through our days. We can tease out of its evolving narrative evidence of sub-lives, parallel existences, omens of shifts that won't be realized for decades, recurrences of themes glimpsed periodically through the years. Learning to read all these things has taught me a respect, bordering on terror, for all that we don't know about our lives. The trail of

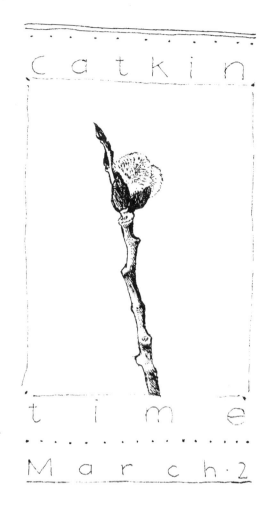

catkin

time

March · 2

words and pictures that I'm leaving is more complete than most people's, but it's still a trail of tips of icebergs, little slices of light and color that are all I can capture of the big masses moving underneath.

But threading through, in fact floating on top of all this matter, like sea ducks among the icebergs, are moments of the ordinary-made-extraordinary by the simple act of choosing and isolating them. I look back to a night in spring twenty years ago, when I stayed up late at the little desk I set up wherever I lived—a sheet of plywood on two orange crates, at which I sat cross-legged on a

SNOWY
FORT

25th

....but as soon as the snowballs become a wall that I hide behind, they _do_ get it.
For awhile it's only Emma & I ———
I lob snowballs, she fields them........

70

Flax
Secret Service

spying

paw through the hole

Emma breaches
the snow fort

watching through
snow fort
hole

71

DRAWING
THE EMERGING
LEAVES ON THE
CLOUDY SPRING
EVENING OF
APRIL TWENTY·FOUR

cushion—drawing the twig of an apple tree just beginning to bloom. The drawing isn't very good, because I tried to add watercolor to it, and I didn't know how to use watercolors then. There are just a few isolated sentences, with lax punctuation. "Apple blossoms coming out full of bees. Most trees with a vapor of tiny green leaves clinging, lawn carpeted with speedwell, warblers returning, nesting beginning. Most lovely pure green leaves not too yellow, trace of fuzz. Blossoms are pink in buds but whiten as petals expand and pink is spread out over a larger area. Lay down under the apple tree in the noon sun, opened my eyes to look up through drifts of blossoms and bees."

I know that I stayed up many nights at that same desk, but the essence of the entire time and place seems to have gathered around the night of that drawing. Just looking at it I can remember the mug of coffee, the jar that held my brushes, and the sound of spring peepers in the nearby pond.

There's nothing special about that night that I recall—no breakthroughs, epiphanies, or raptures. The words were simply dreamy impressions. But something happened there, some powerful gathering force was present, though I didn't know it at the time.

I think the journal itself has taught me to revere the ordinary. For one thing, it was a refuge from trouble and confusion during the profoundly unsettled years, between ages 18 and 24. When you need a safe place, and you find it in a little corner with a book, a pen, and a cup of coffee, you naturally develop a sense of gratitude for the things you associate with safety. They are the ones that seem to anchor your world against vicious and unreadable tides. It was during those hours that I learned to draw the mug, the vase of lilacs, the cat on the rocking chair, the gleaming horse-chestnut, with thankful attention, not to say relief. Looking back through the volumes, I can always tell by the drawings which moments had taken on that restful luminosity. There is a certain stillness, or completion, about them.

Sometimes the general urge to open the book and start writing results in a new look at something, or a conclusion drawn, or a vague thought crystallized; but typically there's just storytelling, describing events in as vivid or funny a way as I can at the moment. The early volumes contain much more soul searching than the current ones do: it took me a long time to find out what kind of a person I would be as an adult. I wanted to be able to wear my self like a useful garment, but I kept turning up in a winter landscape with a cocktail dress on, or in a summer garden with my down coat and snowmobile boots. Now I've managed to put together a versatile little psychic ensemble, appropriate for all occasions, and so can turn my eyes outward without wondering whether my soul is suitably clad.

As a result I have much more time to notice what's in front of me, and illuminate it with affectionate attention. Not that I'm dewily alert all the time: on the contrary, the hours of opacity still outweigh the transparent ones. But I've learned to give more emphasis to, and be more appreciative of, the times when I do surface in the present.

Ironically, moments of wakefulness can occur in the act of facing, (and finding words for) dullness! Here are a few passages from the current volume. You can see that I'm easily entertained, which is one of the simple-minded consequences of coming to dwell more fully in the present.

"For the past week, using the body as a beast of burden or a sort of small-scale wheelbarrow, carting the carcass to and from the studio, into and out of bed."

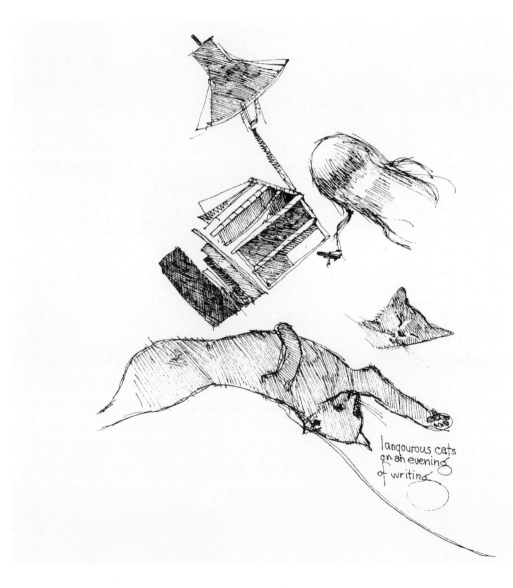

languorous cats on an evening of writing

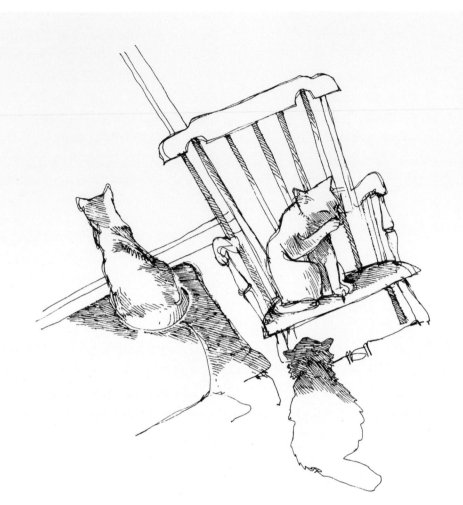

"Haunting the San Juan airport again, during a 5 hour layover. Right now near my seat two young lovers appear to be undergoing a tragic parting (they're on the other side of a glass though, so I can't hear them)—caresses, nuzzles, full-scale embraces, eye-gazing forehead to forehead, whispering. The boy especially seems to be in the latter stages of infatuation. Women are basically more forthright & matter-of-fact about love, believing more fully in the grip of the infant on hip than in the sudden eruption of male tenderness. I can see that 'humoring him' look in her eyes. And here's a dignified young black man embracing a cat-size sky kennel. What can be in it?"

"Have just been scratching the ponies, who now know about the door to the studio, and paw the board outside it, or rattle the doorknob trying to get me to come out. Flax has come to find me too, the ultimate sensual love creature. Now he's climbing around on the shelves trying to get me to notice him, stepping on crackly things & subtly pushing art supplies toward the edges. Bangs are stiff now because ponies love to mouth them. It's Saturday night but I'm too dirty to go out and too lazy to get cleaned up."

"Funny episode of the horses and the hose. It's half frozen but I turn it on, and broken-up cylinders of ice shoot out the end like machine-gun bullets. Horses snort and gallop to the far end of the enclosure."

A delight in the obvious, the daily, still rescues me from dangerous ground, but it's a different landscape of dangers now that I'm middle-aged. Now a year goes by in the same amount of time that a summer vacation did when I was little, and the momentum is increasing. The knowledge that it's slipping away, that it isn't endless, is unsettling to all of us, and can become a subtle kind of poison. Its antidote is to do things that alter time. Drawing does it for me, almost always. So do the puttering tasks involved with gardening (not the terror of transplanting, though). Even shaping words with a favorite pen is sufficient, often. A long, absorbed entry in the journal can also change the tempo. But simply stopping to look at the sky, to watch the colt drinking, to pet the cat and listen to him purr, to smell and savor the coffee as it's brewing—so ordinary as to be beneath notice, and yet containing the seeds of a hardy, perennial joy —those are the acts that knit the world together. The prisoner of war learns about them, too: they are among the few things that can't be taken from him.

Drawing seems to provide an extra measure of engagement. Especially the kind of drawing that pulls you out of yourself, and even off the page, into contemplation of something outside you. It's almost as though, while drawing, we generate a sort of psychic camouflage, becoming still like the surface of a pond when the wind dies down. There

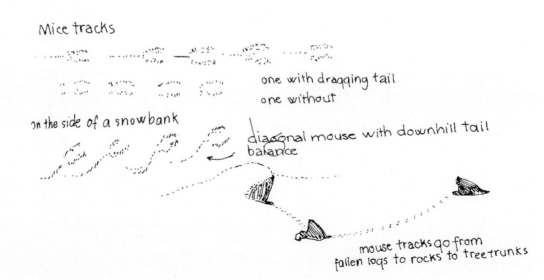

Mice tracks

one with dragging tail
one without

on the side of a snowbank

diagonal mouse with downhill tail
balance

mouse tracks go from
fallen logs to rocks to tree trunks

26 September

Now have three of the seven pens operational, and my hand is beginning to respond again with that most subtle of touches. Pen & hand both require regular exercise to stay in shape. This is the exacting 3 x 0 — mollify it by keeping it in a humidified box. And have finally learned the workings of the humidifier arrangement on my drawing table.

Bob Reich was nice enough to bring over a couple of dozen eggs from their chickens — ecstatic to see fertile eggs again — hard shells: the crack of the eggs of my childhood — warm brown color, small, distinct, shapely yolks of brilliant yellow, that keep themselves intact until you really whip them up.

Egg alphabet — egg shaped LETTERS......

Created an omelet with six of them — could've eaten 8 — plus the addition of a fresh tomato, fresh cilantro & chives, two kinds of cheese & sour cream & salsa as topping

gorgeous · gangbusters · gangly · ganglion · glug · giggle · gaggle

is something in the world that is pleased when we do that, that steals up behind us then. We feel it as an increased clarity, as a hush, as a kind of music, or an animation. A poem by Theodore Roethke that I discovered many years ago still suggests what this enchantment is like:

"It was beginning winter"
It was beginning winter,
An in-between time,
The landscape still partly brown:
The bones of weeds kept swinging in the wind,
Above the blue snow.
It was beginning winter,
The light moved slowly over the frozen field,
Over the dry seed crowns,

The beautiful surviving bones
Swinging in the wind.
Light traveled over the wide field;
Stayed.
The weeds stopped swinging.
The mind moved, not alone,
Through the clear air, in the silence.
　　Was it light?
　　Was it light within?
　　Was it light within light?
　　Stillness becoming alive,
　　Yet still?
A lively understandable spirit
Once entertained you.
It will come again.
Be still.
Wait.

We are restless creatures, easily bored, and demons regularly fill our
vacancies. A journal-keeper, whose subject is his life, has to face
daily his inability to be satisfied. The Zen precept that directs us
to "chop wood, carry water" means that by being as awake and present as possible, during even the most mundane acts, we can
arrest the restlessness. Daily life and patterns
of habit tend to obscure our appreciation for
what's right in front of us. Use the journal to
rediscover your most intimate surroundings, to
give thanks for small pleasures.

Take a tour of your house or apartment, making small drawings as you go.
Visit the places in this dwelling that always
please you, and make a note of why they
do. Where do you spend most of your time?
What do you do there? Make a sketch of that
place.

Also, seek out some part of the house you
never, or rarely visit or pay any attention to.
Describe what's going on there.

Find a place where the sun is coming
through a window, and draw what it falls on. Pay
special attention to the shapes of the shadows.

Find something odd or funny in your home;
draw it and describe it.

Draw a favorite workspace, just as it is, and describe everything that's within
view, down to yesterday's coffee mug, and the crunched-up piece of paper that
represents a false start.

Draw a pet, a plant, a child, a mate, a friend, a relative who is at ease in your
home.

As a way of cultivating an appreciation of the overlooked ordinary, do some writing in your journal about moments of common contentment. How about the sensation of sinking into a comfortable bed at night, or of stretching in the morning under covers that are the ideal temperature? Or the awareness in the middle of a jog that your body is working smoothly, that you are entertained by everything you see? The smell of your favorite soap in the shower, your dog's delighted greeting when you've been away for a while. The comfort of falling asleep in the embrace of someone you love.

Some of the moments are repeated regularly, so regularly that they fade into the background and out of awareness, the way city people cease to hear traffic noise. Your task is to bring them back into awareness, and acknowledge them as the gifts they are.

Some strike suddenly, in the midst of something so mundane as raking the leaves, or braking for a stoplight. Recall a few of those moments when you felt inexplicably happy, and the thoughts and actions associat-ed with them, and write about them.

For several days, limit the entries in your journal to bare-bones descriptions of things you really *saw*. For today, I have a fairly long list already, and it's only noon: the new leaf the palm tree is putting out, a really big one; the frost left in exactly the shape of the shadow of the house; two of my cats taking luxurious dustbaths in the driveway; the look of the manure breaking up in the corral into glorious veg-etable matter, soon to be plowed under; the colt's curious face as he followed me around while I raked; the silvery green nubbins at the base of the fringe-sage, and the tiny leaves of catnip coming up through last year's dead debris. This way of writing teaches you a new focus. If your journal entries now consist mostly of

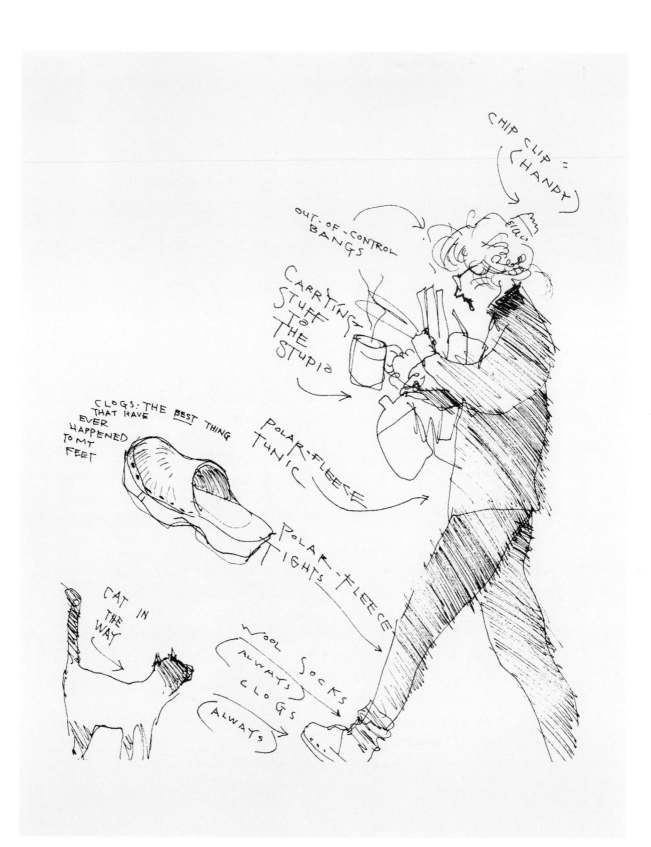

complaints, analysis, fretting over personalities, envy or worry, turn this simple accounting into a daily practice.

When you cook, pay attention to the ancient ritual you are enacting. Bake some bread, and make sketches of every stage of the process. Draw your favorite vegetables and fruits. After breakfast, draw the dishes and crusts, as a memento of a basic act of starting the day.

If you play a musical instrument, draw it, and describe what you're currently practicing. Draw your favorite pen, your favorite bowl, your favorite shoes, the contents of your purse, your favorite knife. Draw a windowsill and its contents. Draw your car, or your bicycle, or your canoe. Draw your trowel, your hat, the view from your window. Drawing something is showing deference for it, investing it with significance.

Make a series of drawings that illustrates a typical day, from your memory and imagination. Try not to select the usual categories, but some of the odd and overlooked things you habitually do. Instead of noting that you get out of bed, show yourself turning on the radio or grinding the coffee beans, or gazing out the window.

Practice turning unpleasant events into funny ones. Once I announced that I'd provide a special dessert for an international dinner. It required caramelizing a cup of sugar and a little water over low heat, a process that was supposed to take about fifteen minutes. I was still watching the dry sugar turn brown an hour later. Finally, grudgingly, it melted into a viscous syrup, walnut brown, that hardened instantly into a plate of glasslike material when I poured it into a pan, though it still *looked* liquefied.

Obviously there wasn't going to be any dessert, but I brought the solid slab of stuff to the party anyway. We marveled at it, then put it on the bathroom floor where it caused a stir among late-arriving guests. I might have been embarrassed, or angry, or frustrated, but this was too good to pass up, and it made a diverting journal entry, complete with illustration. And just last year, I was able to turn a bout with the 24-hour flu into something that made me laugh the whole time I was writing about it (after the fact).

COLORADO MOUNTAINS

Oh god how lovely — a meadow with aspens some gold, some white and fawn colored grass, deep evergreens. I'm sitting against a rock in aspen leaves & sage, waiting for the elk to bugle.

Far off, still high in the mountains we hear a great cry !!!! They are coming down!

Next time you have a truly foul day, transform it in the journal by emphasizing the ridiculous, the idiotic, the absurd. After a few attempts at this, you'll be mining the most miserable and difficult moments for their comic potential.

There is an unspoken mantra that runs through me all day, a kind of prompting that reminds me to disengage from the maelstrom every so often. It encourages me to pause and look around on my way from the house to the studio—that's when I see my colt stretching just like a dog or cat, something I never knew horses did. If the mantra had words, it would say something like: "*Here I am, alive, right now*". . . a steady, quiet wake-up call. The journal is the embodiment and the continuation of that mantra.

In it there's also an undertone that says nothing is really ordinary and familiar after all; that all this I see basking in the light of dailiness could be, and will be, gone tomorrow. As the thirteenth-century poet Kabir said, "You have slept for millions and millions of years. Why not wake up this morning?"

Chapter 5

THE FLOW OF ATTENTION

A fan of drainages lies to the north of me, all tributaries of Wind River. They penetrate a sea of cliffs, canyons, and plateaus of volcanic origin, hundreds of square miles, some of the wildest country in the lower forty-eight, if these little islands can truly be called wild anymore. It's is a stronghold of the grizzly, a place of mystery. Compared to the badlands and the sage plains in the valley, which get along on about ten inches of moisture a year, some spots up in the Absarokas attract sixty inches, fostering a lush paradise of grasses and gentians, boglets and little trout-teeming runnels. Freak thunderstorms are known to pile up at the head of one rib of this fan: a geologist friend of mine, whose lifelong study has been the southern wall of the Absarokas, has found enormous washouts, evidence of torrential downpours on a singular scale.

I have only a few hours to walk today; all I can do is drive up to the old Dennison place, a long-abandoned dude ranch that was once one of Wyoming's most glamorous, and climb from there. This is the broken foothills belt; a jumble of cliffs, boulder-studded meadows, hidden grassy pockets; my geologist friend dubbed it "the chaos zone." The trees, especially on south-facing hillsides, are crabbed old lightning-maimed limber pines and junipers, many only half alive, their dead sections riddled by cavities that in summer house flickers and bluebirds. The quiet and the light here, especially in fall, have a sad, lost, distant quality that is just what I crave at the moment.

Early this morning, with a good cup of coffee, in the chilly studio, I wrote a long entry in the journal, at intervals working on a sketch on the facing page while waiting for thoughts to form. I was expecting a lively account of all the little events of the last few days, a varied but typical mix of solitary work, outings, dinners and conversations with friends, notes on the weather and the progress of the season, comments on animals, woodchopping, and bulb catalogues, with maybe a few moments of insight about life and its workings.

What I got instead was an upheaval of fury, discouragement, and fear that I had not known was just beneath the surface. It was pervaded by the troubling atmosphere of a dream, now past retrieval, except for a memory of looming, threatening figures. Anything else I attempted in the next hours would, I knew, lead me into a dead-end alley of hopelessness, so I decided to hand my grim attitude over to natural conditions. Either I would return buffeted, soothed, recharged, unchanged, or in some as yet unencountered state.

So I'm driving up the long rough road to Bear Creek and the Dennison place, seeking a spot that will suit this eruption of melancholy. I hope to find out more about what undercurrents are present, and what they mean. At times, it's better to go at such murky and elusive things by a less than direct route, the way you can see a dim star better if you look slightly to one side. Or the way, if you hope to observe a grizzly without disturbing it, you better do it from a long distance, through a spotting scope.

So, for now, no music, no books on tape, no prescribed thoughts, just the smell of the dust on the road and an eye that always roams hungrily

over the contours of the landscape, independent of moods and humors. Attention doesn't necessarily follow the eye, in fact it seems that they operate independently much of the time. We like to think of them as working in unison, we demand it for reading, writing, and conversation, but a certain kind of disjointedness or dissociation between them is a symptom, for me at least, of creativity at work.

I find I want to learn more about the vagaries of attention, and, paradoxically, try to track them. I relish using the skill of focused attention, but believe, increasingly, that we need to grant consequence to the less directed chunks of awareness,

too. Attention wanders far more widely than most of us realize. Just how flimsy is our conviction that there is a unified "I" that is the active thinker of our thoughts? The "I" can't be a fiction, but it may be a less defined, or a more inclusive structure than we assume it is.

Attention moves in wide-ranging intuitive movements, from interior to exterior and back, like a wolf hunting over a big territory. Even when we consider ourselves to be "paying attention," it continues to make half-secret excursions, as though it has its own dens to visit and scent posts to mark. Many of these excursions never register on consciousness. We have disciplined ourselves to con-

1.5

SLABS
OF
LIMESTONE

MOST
CHARCOAL COLOR,
SOME PALE GRAY

SAND
IVORY

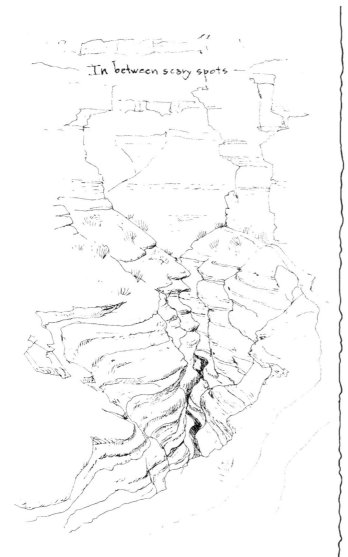

In between scary spots —

centrate, to ignore detours that may be frightening, or to dismiss them as "nonsense."

Consequently, our impression of our own interior lives might be an elaborate falsehood; we imagine that we stay within the familiar pasture when really our attention is out roaming the talus slopes and snowfields. We convince ourselves that the life of the mind is a well-husbanded field with clear boundaries, even though we know there's a howling waste not far beyond the fence.

As a journal-keeper looking at a blank page, I

wait to see what attention will light on, what will be winnowed from the legions of seed-thoughts out there. It can be frustrating to watch the harvest being sifted through restrictive screens: chronological time, rational narrative, familiar space, limited characters. Too many rare and extraordinary seeds are discarded. The result is a more coherent record, but not necessarily a real one.

To follow the actual workings of attention, and watch what it does when it thinks it isn't being watched, I have to be willing to go into dark places, and like most of us, I'm afraid—that way lies madness, and we shy away from it as though sensing how close to disintegration the self really is. But if we insist on staying in the well-lighted places, we never learn the full range of the territory, and become more susceptible to sudden ambushes from the darkness.

When scoffers refer to meditation as "navel gazing," I know what they are picturing: someone indulging in congratulatory self-reflection. Journal-keepers come in for the same criticism. In my experience, both practices (which are close relatives) tend to have the opposite effect. They lead out of the self and back to the world, or, it might be better to say, knit the two into one fabric. The detachment required for meditation worthy of its name, and for journal entries that are fearless and lucid, creates a healthy uncertainty about the self. Meditators and journal-keepers have come to know and respect its feral nature, and are far less likely to be complacent and self-satisfied. They know they are dealing with something undomesticated.

My local bookstore is stocked with books about meditation techniques that can coax out of hiding the true shape of attention. I'd vote for solitary walking. Stepping outside the comfortable padding of books, music, news, movies, magazines, conversations, all the reassuring attention-absorbers, is a necessary act of exposure. In fact, removing all of that padding must be one of our deepest fears, judging by the enormous amount of ingenuity we've employed over the centuries to keep from doing it. The art of making something from nothingness is our greatest virtue, and we can't and shouldn't try to thwart it, but at times, to stay awake, we need to leave the swaddling behind.

I park the truck near an old corral, and step out into the poised hush of a November afternoon. Shadows from the western wall are already reaching into the big meadow, with the peculiar intensity of color that vibrates along their edges, a penumbral waver that I always perceive as both blue-violet and reddish brown. There are two moose within the shadow, a mother and a big calf, who are watching me with slow moosely apprehension. I turn my back on them and walk toward the trees, as a way of putting them at ease. It's quite cold in the patch of forest between two cliffs—the unmelted snow is a blue that has never known sum-

mer—and for a while I simply try to find my way back into my body. I need to let it get used to moving, wait for the reliable blood-pumping flush that will banish the cold.

I'm prepared for the barrage of mind-chatter that is thrown into relief against the natural emptiness. The mind seems stupidly busy, darting mouse-like at one thought after another, few of them useful, few even completed. Eyes are equally busy, but I already know that colors will remain just colors and forms ordinary and familiar for at least an hour after I set out walking. To look at— to really see—the dead flower stalks of sagebrush quivering in the impersonal wind would be unbearable this soon, too steeped in loneliness. Instead my eyes scan the landscape with a purposeful motion that feels suspiciously like reading. That kind of looking is exhausting; it's the reason for the weariness that we feel after hours in a museum.

The rhythm of walking is soothing, it cradle-rocks the mind, allowing thoughts to unfold and mature in a less harried way. But attention still roams distractedly, remembering the past and envisioning the future, running as though long confined, uncovering things in no particular order. While mind's-eye pictures prevail, I'm not fully inhabiting the landscape. Inner images and language dissolve, returning me to the present moment and the actual ground I'm walking on— with a sensation of surfacing, as though I had been underwater—then I submerge again.

Switchbacking up a hillside, I keep an eye on the cliffs that are my objective. Now attention leaves its inward circling to monitor the body, which is working too hard to ignore. It takes note of the heart thudding and breath quickening, of the ache

CROAKING RAVENS · SOUNDS LIKE A DIALOGUE

TINY RILL TRINKLINGS · SMALL DRIPS OVER SMALL STONE·

CLARK'S NUTCRACKER WINGBEATS

CAN FEEL SHADOWS LENGTHENING

ONE OF THOSE LITTLE WINTER SPARROW CHIPS

in thigh muscles and knees, of sweat under my headband. I've learned to like the feeling of working hard, but it's not the goal of this walk, so I slow down and focus on achieving a steady breathing rate. The mind, the attention, have become more

If I stay out long enough, I can expect this transition, though it doesn't always happen. Colors become more distinct and saturated, light more radiant and dense, even on cloudy days. The blasted trunk of a limber pine beside me, which I would only have glanced at a while ago, glows now with a vivid marbling of lavender-gray and burnt orange, and the dead bunch-grasses are no longer just pale, but suffused with gold. It's not just that the colors have become more beautiful; now they have a peculiar rightness, a perfection, and their combinations seem at once startlingly rich and subtle. How could I have missed the silver-copper

cow parsnip

tractable by now, like a good horse when it leaves behind the prancing and head-tossing and settles into a steady pace.

After an hour, thought-journeys into past and future have become less compulsive, and less tinged with regret and anxiety. As I reach the little notch that will bring me to the top of the cliff, I realize that my eyes have abandoned their aggressive "reading," and have begun to do what I can only call "caress" things. They linger on the graininess of this shelf of sandstone, and admire the sheen coming from the mica in it. At the top of the cliff I stop, and find that I've crossed the color threshold.

of the pearly everlasting, under my feet all this time? There is even a hint of a warm rosiness at its heart, felt rather than seen, precisely.

Now I know, strolling out across the rolling flank of the mountain, that ahead of me lies a solid period of sensory pleasure. I don't know how long it will last. Metabolism usually determines its duration, if time isn't a factor. At this point it's best to drop into a wander, with only a vague direction or perhaps a landmark to steer by.

It might be that the eyes make an adjustment analogous to the expansion and contraction of the pupil, only for color instead of light. I associate crossing the color threshold with exercise. Perhaps it's due to a general enrichment of oxygen in the bloodstream, which in turn boosts the performance of the cone cells, the ones responsible for color perception. In any case it's something that I look forward to, and revel in while it lasts. Sometimes, even when I'm not in that state, I can conjure up the sense of how perfectly certain colors go together just by remembering how they appeared when I had crossed the color threshold.

Today, along with a heightened awareness of light and color, comes a rinse of relief: I have arrived here, all is well. Time and events are no longer fragmented and jostling, alternately blurred and distinct. I no longer have the sensation of traveling down corridors of thought and entering isolated rooms of memory and projection, then struggling to return to the present. It's as though all the selves and their contents have come out in the open, revealed in a wide, gracious space.

And since all is revealed and accessible, however briefly, I can listen to the voice that spoke distress in the journal this morning. Several things fall into place, and with no fanfare, a sort of solution

appears, or at least a course of action. The forgotten, poisonous dream comes a little closer: I can match its atmosphere of dread to a cluster of exchanges and situations over the last half-year that carried the same dread: too much misplaced openness, followed by invasion, followed by retreat, and then new attempts at openness. A change is wanted, but it's not the change of resolve, rather the subtle shift that results when lucidity replaces bafflement. There's a little click, like the knob of a dislocated joint slipping back into its housing.

I spot twelve bighorn sheep bedded down on a golden slope in the last of the sun, and sink down

Lake Champlain
interlude —

lapping wavelets
slowly building thunderstorm · south
gulls crying
smooth warm limestone bedrock
distant & more distant forested shores
spotted sandpiper
the frog on the rock
our arbor vitae room
chipunks almost trampling us
deep forest — oaks· white pines
another mystery pine
vireo song
windless, still water

5pm

93

against a boulder to share a few moments of rest with them, before turning back. They see me; the ram is mildly watchful, but I recognize the faint motion of jaws in rumination, so I know he isn't disturbed.

With a little distance from both pain and rapture, I remember that the miracle in all this is that there is a self at all: that these senses coordinate and add up to awareness, lodged in no particular place in the brain, but rather a super-function involving the whole. There is an irreducible integrity in this, an innate excellence, and I'm suddenly full of gratitude, toward what or whom I don't know, just to be one of the elect, a soul awake in the world. This has nothing to do with accomplishment, or goodness, or will; it's the gift common to everything alive.

Still, pain is the hidden framework of aware-

ness, built into it, in the same way that space is a prerequisite for time to exist. Death, fear, and loss are inescapable; it's when we experience them as an individually designed hell that we writhe most pathetically under them. My journal entry of this morning showed fear looping back on itself, into fear of the fear and dread of the dread, a sort of persecution seizure. Such a morass is best dealt with by allowing it to surface, then standing back to let it do the work it has to do.

The sky has taken on that late dusk transparency, so I gather up binoculars and water bottle and strap on the pack again, over a down vest. I'm glad even to be on the fringes of a great empty territory, a place that doesn't belong to us. To penetrate its wild heart requires serious preparation, and lots of time, so that's a once-or-twice a year event for me. Most often I'm treading its margins, always

1. Blonde flatiron hills, one of the series that extends the length of the range

2. Benchlike levels also repeated throughout the range

3. Canyon bottom, nearly flat

4. Beginnings of evergreen clad foothills

aware of the miles and days of wildness just over the ridge.

And I don't really want to know its heart as well as I know my own back yard. I want it to be unfamiliar, not an extension of my usual trails. I want that strange, rain-attracting upland to remain unpredictable and potent, distant and dangerous, sending down its freak torrents; the remote, snow-laden source of summer water. I want to know that there are undomesticated animals out there, with huge ranges, equal to any conditions, who live and move without restraint.

Journal-keepers as a species are likely to have a better notion of where their attention is at any given moment than most people: they are used to transcribing at least a few of its rambles whenever they open the book, and from that they gain a sense of its habits. Betty Edwards, in *Drawing on the Right Side of the Brain*, describes a perceptual shift that occurs when we draw. If the analytical left side of the brain, the one that wants to identify, classify, and move on to the next thing, is induced to give up its hold on consciousness for a while, the intuitive, sense-grounded right brain is released to create.

In this dual-brain theory (which has a lot of research to back it up) the left brain's strengths are language, symbols, and abstraction; it is content to let a stick figure represent a person, and doesn't want to look at nameless shapes and lights and shadows. The right brain excels in seeing likenesses between things, in recognizing overall patterns; it doesn't keep track of time and doesn't work sequentially. A stick figure doesn't satisfy the right brain; it wants the real-life body.

Betty Edwards is happy to see the left brain subdued when we draw, at least until we've found our way into the work. Later it can serve a useful function in some drawings, when assessment and analysis are required. When the hand, the

eye, and the visual mind are engaged in drawing, the left brain drops into the background, but it's still active. In much the same way as solitary walking, the act of drawing takes pressure off the word-making mind and lets it idle and play.

Try launching into a sustained drawing. Choose something to draw that has lots of intricate but repetitive details, or big areas of tone and texture. The seed stalk of a hollyhock would be good, or the facade of an ornate building. You'll need focused attention to build the framework of the drawing, but as soon as you have placed things in a way that satisfies you, it will be time to begin fleshing out the drawing, using many small lines, dots, cross-hatching, or slowly built-up areas of tone or color.

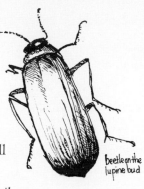
beetle on the
lupine bud

Reserve part of the page spread for words. As you settle into the drawing, you'll notice that out of that quiet work, thoughts and images float to the surface, usually not demanding attention for themselves; they appear in the background, and at first they will be hard to register. Casually, without breaking the mood of the drawing, shift your hand to the word space, and jot down very briefly, paying no attention at all to grammar or syntax, only the substance of the thought or image. And just as smoothly, resume the drawing. When the next thought-event occurs, slip over and get it down. Don't worry about whether the thoughts are connected, coherent, or related to anything important. Right now, you simply want to be gathering them as they come within range.

At first you will feel resistance to switching back and forth between these two activities. One of two things will happen: either you won't want to break the rhythm of the drawing and will effectively tune out thoughts surfacing in the background, or, when you turn to transcribe, the language mind will invade and compel you to keep writing, even though you've already gotten down the germ of the thought.

What's valuable to me about this practice is that it recognizes the discrete nature of thoughts: they aren't necessarily linked in a consistent flow, and they arrive on their own schedule. When we write, we often force thoughts into contrived sequences, rejectingbranch-thoughts because they don't contribute directly to the narrative under construction. Here, we're taking things down just as they are delivered, and then leaving them alone.

Transcriptions may come in little bursts, with long periods of absorbed drawing between. Or they may come in steadily, like waves breaking. This drawing-thinking process suggests that thoughts travel along like schools of porpoises, under the water and invisible much of the time, but surfacing regularly. Where you spotted them last won't necessarily tell you where they'll come up next time.

Later, when you have finished the draw-ing, look over the transcriptions. Sometimes the connections among them will remain opaque, to be appreciated simply as a grab-bag assortment. Other times a hidden progression, theme, or question becomes apparent. Whichever hap-pens, you are left with an authentic raw document that might contain more than 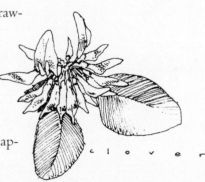 you can absorb at the moment. If you're intrigued by what shows up in the words, allow some time to amplify in writing. Ask more questions now, while the thoughts are still fresh.

If you are curious enough to want to find out what your attention does all day, to track it set your watch, or a little timer, to ring every hour, or two hours. Whenever it rings, open the journal and write down briefly what you were doing and how your mind was occupied when the timer caught you. There will be moments when you can't write, of course: try carrying one of those little tape recorders, and then add your spoken comments to the journal later. To extend the experiment, you might take a reading on your mood, alertness, and energy

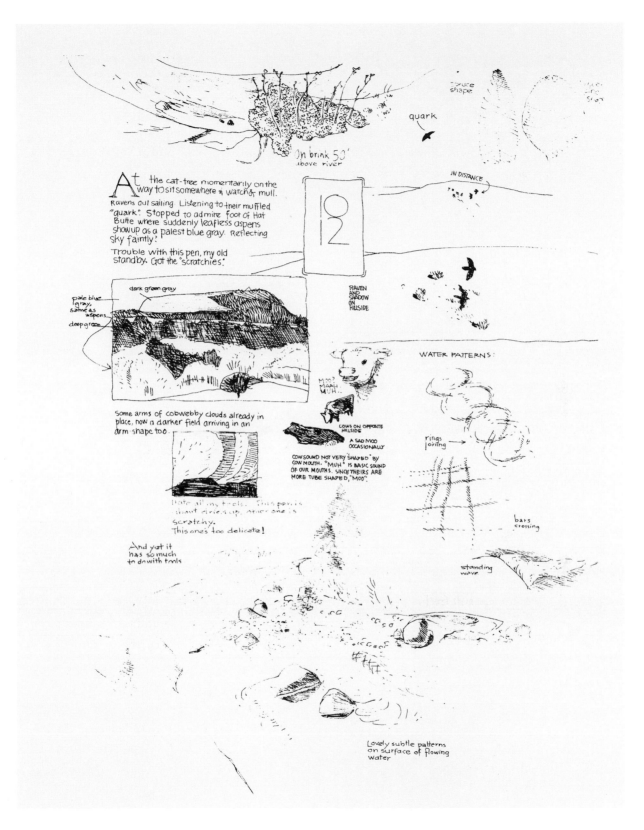

quark

spruce shape

On brink 50' above river

IN DISTANCE

At the cat-tree momentarily on the way to sit somewhere & watch & mull.

Ravens out sailing. Listening to their muffled "quark". Stopped to admire foot of Hat Butte where suddenly leafless aspens show up as a palest blue gray. Reflecting sky faintly?

Trouble with this pen, my old standby. Got the "scratchies".

RAVEN AND SHADOW ON HILLSIDE

dark green gray

pale blue gray, same as aspens

deep green

WATER PATTERNS:

Some arms of cobwebby clouds already in place, now a darker field arriving in an arm-shape too.

MOO? MAAH MUH.

COWS ON OPPOSITE HILLSIDE

A SAD MOO OCCASIONALLY

COW SOUND NOT VERY "SHAPED" BY COW MOUTH. "MUH" IS BASIC SOUND OF OUR MOUTHS. SINCE THEIRS ARE MORE TUBE SHAPED, "MOO".

rings joining

bars crossing

Hate all my tools. This pen is about dried up, other one is scratchy.
This one's too delicate!

And yet it has so much to do with tools

standing wave

Lovely subtle patterns on surface of flowing water

Sensations

Nauseating hot flash feel of clouds of sulphurous steam on face ......

And the pleasure of watching Mustard Spring retreat into its hole, then start to become restless again... would have been satisfied to watch that process for a good several hours.

But what's wrong? Why no words? Why no delight in getting them wrapped around an image?

Words are the way emotions find outlet in you.

Feelings are such right now —

—that you don't really want to get too close to the words, too close to the brink.

anxiety, apprehension, exhaustion, discouragement

Emotions are boiling springs, ready to cook & disintegrate.

Yet there's the relief of having said something abt it, yes?

Yes. Not such a hidden hold now.

Just another malleable condition.

Drops reflect world upside down? No, just curved, I think

That the water plops are stretched by air pressure and when they stretch enough then drops break off, some quite large...

DROPS WAY DOWN INTO ITS HOLE THEN EVERY FEW MINUTES RISES UP & STARTS SPOUTING

100

level with each entry. If you are truly dedicated, wake yourself up several time in the course of a night, just to see if you can snare a dream.

This kind of day-long entry creates an unusual cross-section of a lived life, especially if you make sure the few sentences you write each time are concrete. Instead of, "I was making dinner for Mike and the kids and thinking about the garden," you can get more specific and say, "I was slicing a tomato, noticing that it's a pleasure to cut with a sharp knife, and thinking about how it will feel to dig up the herb bed."

As a way of keeping the flavor of these two methods alive in your regular journal-keeping, try a series of notations that will allow you at least to acknowledge the thought-trails branching off from the main path of an entry. Numbers, letters, lines pulled out to the side, addendums on the edges of the page: devise a way to point in the direction of the "road not taken" at important junctures, so that so much material isn't sacrificed to the demands of unity and logic.

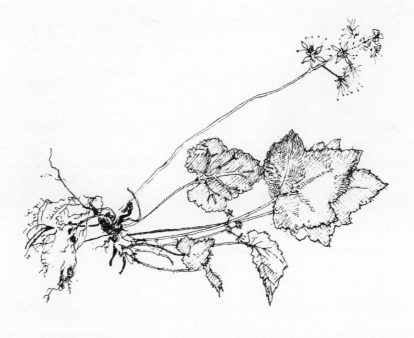

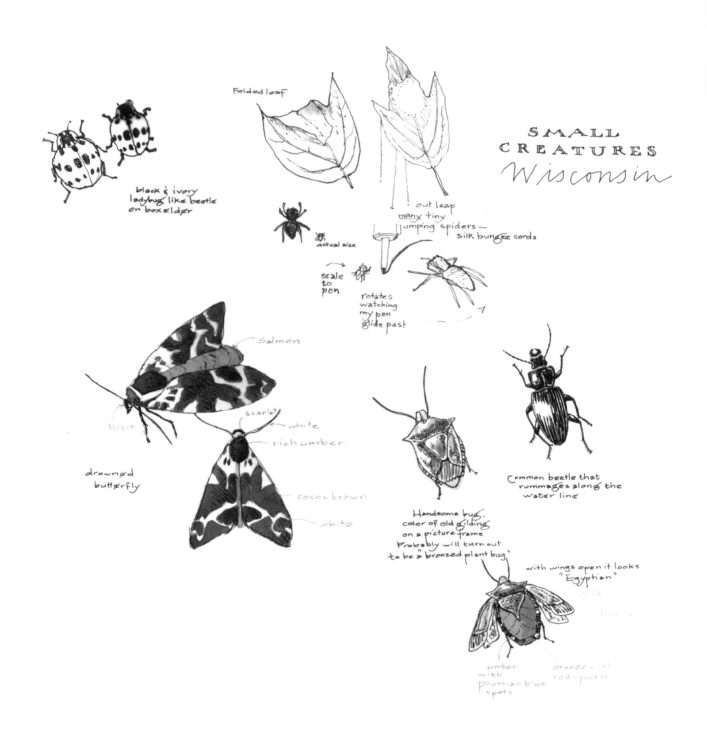

black & ivory
ladybug like beetle
on boxelder

Folded leaf

SMALL
CREATURES
Wisconsin

out leap
<u>many</u> tiny
jumping spiders —
silk bungee cords

actual size

scale
to
pen

rotates
watching
my pen
glide past

Salmon

scarlet
white
rich umber

Black

drowned
butterfly

cocoa brown

white

Common beetle that
rummages along the
water line

Handsome bug.
color of old gilding
on a picture frame
Probably will turn out
to be a "bronzed plant bug"

with wings open it looks
"Egyptian"

umber
with
prussian blue
spots

orange with
red spots

Chapter 6

SEEING ORDER, SEEING CHAOS

One night many years ago on a summer evening, I sat on the top rail of a fence and looked out over pastures to the dense wall of woods that edged them. A few lightning bugs had begun to signal, and I watched them, wondering if it was just a coincidence that they appeared to be flying upward every time they flashed.

The air over the field grew dense with the little insects, and as I watched, a pattern within the blinking began to suggest itself. It looked as though the lightning bugs were firing sequentially; I could pick out long lines of them apparently doing just that, the way the blinking lights in a movie marquee give the impression of rapid movement. At first the effect was so convincing that I had to question seriously whether the lightning bugs had somehow worked out such a flash pattern as part of their signaling ritual.

It seemed more likely that what I was seeing was an optical, or rather a perceptual illusion. My eyes

and brain, without conscious prompting, had supplied an arrangement for the random firings, identifying an interval of about a third of a second, and linking the flashes in any direction. Once I interpreted my vision that way, it became easier and easier to pick out these sequences, so that they flowed almost continuously, adding a thrilling but imaginary urgency to the mating display of the little creatures.

On the way back to the cabin I picked a stalk of foxglove from the garden and brought it inside, placing it in the water jug that sat on the drawing table, which was covered with illustrations of ducks and duck plumages. I wondered what made the foxglove so visually appealing. I first considered its symmetry and regularity, but then decided that what I liked best to examine was the tip of the stem, where the buds diminish in size; smaller and smaller versions of the basic foxglove pattern, but more and more appealingly unformed at the tip. So

The Owl
February 24
that I found hit on the road back from Lander Saturday, just after dawn. Only neck broken. Still warm. Many owls hunt on roads, watching for animals to cross or picking up snakes that seek roads for warmth.

strong, stretchy web of skin that joins wing to body

ears are parallel with eyes, right behind facial disks

on the 40 minute drive from Crowheart, where I found him, kept petting him, feeling his talons which at that point were relaxed and flexible. In fact, entwining my hand in one talon, half-consciously trying to warm it. Feeling the texture of the "palm" of the talon, and all the different kinds of feathers.

facial disk feathers are stiff bristles black tipped when they emerge here

fan of bristle feathers & moustache bleak — turn to short, very soft feathers under chin and on throat

lower mandible has a little notch where it fits against upper

the attraction was partly scale, the pleasure we all knew from opening those nesting Russian dolls, each tinier than the last, yet retaining form and detail. And it was partly development: that I could see all the stages, from bud to mature blossom, on the same stem.

Glancing at the plumage paintings, it was suddenly obvious that I had not been paying attention to scale: the white spots on the breast of a wood duck are arranged very much like the blossoms of a foxglove. The small spots are close together, and as they progress to bigger spots, the distance between them grows proportionately. I'd tried to paint the spots in rows, but had missed the cadenced way the pattern changes. And something like development was going on in the spot pattern, too. The bigger ones were distinctly shaped, while the smaller ones retained a bud-like quality.

The events of that night were aptly paired: first, my pattern-hungry mind *imposed* order on randomness, in the lightning bug marquee. Next I *uncovered* pattern in the relation of foxglove to wood duck, where I had missed it before. Because I have a sketchy account in my journal of that night, I know that my interest in pattern, scale, and design in nature dates to about that time. Since then, I've made a game of searching out the ordering princi-

ples that underlie natural phenomena; wanting to know them also forms the core of my deepest urges to draw. The fit of the order-seeking mind to the order-filled universe seems to me one of the best "givens" we have to work with.

Patterns, textures, designs in nature can be enjoyed just for themselves. I don't have to analyze the foxglove to find it beautiful. But once you have experienced the "ah ha!" of discovering why something looks the way it does, you can't stop peeling back the layers. It's deeply satisfying to

discover a link between form and function, the how and the why.

It took me a long time to realize, for instance, that spruce branches are arranged in spiral whorls around the trunk, and that the pattern is repeated in the cones, whose seeds are also arranged in spirals. I learned much later the name for this phenomenon: spiral phyllotaxis. Different plant groups have evolved a whole catalog of methods for filling space efficiently. Keeping this principle in mind while studying and drawing plants and flowers in the field, the journal-keeper can discover how each kind has solved the problem.

In the woods I've often picked up strange bits of decaying pine and spruce trees. At first I regarded them as curiosities, then realized that I was holding parts of old branches that had been engulfed by the expanding trunk of the tree. Where the trunk has to part to flow around the branch is

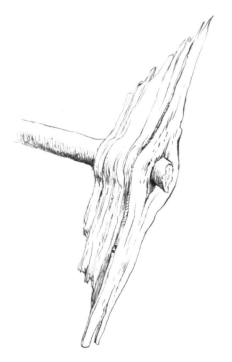

where the wood is most compressed, forming tough knots that make splitting branchy wood so difficult. Old branches, with some of this dense trunk wood surrounding them, are often the very last parts of a dead tree to decay. You may find them on the ground around the ghost of an old fallen tree, more impervious to weather and rot than the spongier parts of the trunk. In this case, there was a story to be unraveled out of an oddity. The fact that I pieced it together for myself made the discovery even more compelling.

And then there is the matter of streams and rivers, and the ways they move across the landscape and over time. After I learned about the meander cycle in geology class, I started to see it everywhere, and still delight in spotting abandoned meanders and oxbow ponds. I've made a collection of sketches in the journal of river patterns and drainage forms as seen from the air. Just this year, flying over St. Louis, I was able to add one of the best yet: meanders on a scale larger than I'd ever seen before, so immense that they couldn't possibly be understood from ground level, miles across, some of the ancient ones marked only by a darker color of soil.

The meander cycle goes something like this, if the stream in question occupies a wide enough valley: Water, of course, is too fluid and variable to flow in a straight line without turbulence, so you may think of the river as beginning with a gentle S curve. As the river begins digging away on the outside of the curves where the current is fastest, and depositing its load of sediment on the inside of the curves where the current is slowest, the S curve gets more and more exaggerated, so that the loops begin to fold back on themselves. After a while there is a very short space between one bend and

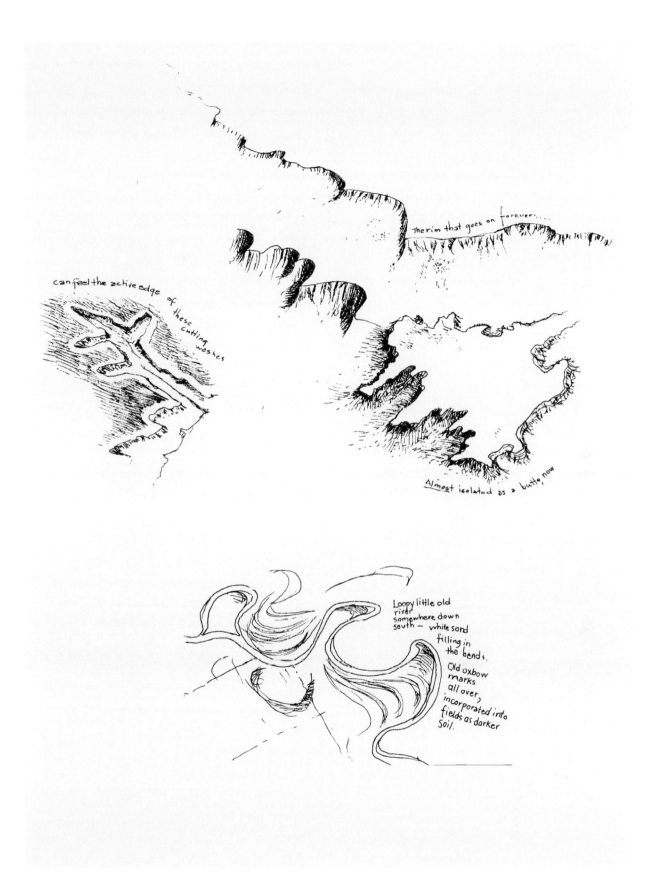

The rim that goes on forever...

can feel the active edge of these cutting washes

Almost isolated as a butte, now

Loopy little old river somewhere down south — white sand filling in the bends.

Old oxbow marks all over, incorporated into fields as darker soil.

107

another, which is eventually cut away completely, and that stretch of river is once again as straight as it's able to be. The bypassed curve, an oxbow, might hold water for quite a while, and be replenished when the river floods.

It's a marvelous poem just as it is. Hydrologists know many more verses to it; profiling the life histories of a huge cast of streams and rivers they can flesh the tale into an epic. A journal-keeper can study the physical permutations of flowing water, or can decide to see the river as analog or metaphor.

The river goes through a stage of complication, when it could be thought to be out of balance. Its energy is going into enormous loops, wider and wider, with more urgent digging on the one side and a huge burden of sediment sloughing off on the other. It isn't making much forward progress, vacillating between extremes instead. Then, either a catastrophic event occurs, like a flood, to straighten out the wildest loops, or the digging itself provides the way to a simpler path. All of us know meander people, and we also know the straight-ahead kind.

The meander cycle is analogous to the way people conduct their lives, and on some level, it mirrors the paths of all of our lives from time to time, with different levels of exaggeration. The journal is the perfect place to try out analogies between natural and human-life processes. Since we're all made of essentially the same stuff, it makes sense that we should share some of the same properties.

In this light I can rethink the pine and spruce knots and the way they were formed. The oldest branches, springing from the original heart of the tree, can be compared with childhood experiences, and first attempts at growth. The expanding trunk

engulfing the old branches corresponds with the accumulation of years. The oldest branches are the ones most surrounded by heartwood, but they may still continue to grow and provide some nourishment for the tree, or they may drop off, leaving a scar.

Generally the wounds of lost branches heal over, but in some trees, like aspens, the marks of the loss never disappear. (And of course the aspen's bark looks and is more sensitive than, say, the corrugated old skin of a cottonwood). By this measure, we should be able to say that the earliest experiences, and the way they shaped the time that accommodated them, and toughened around them, are the most persistent parts of the person.

Poets live and breathe this kind of thinking. I'm not a poet, and I'm usually content to let the tree be a tree without burdening it with metaphor. But if, by becoming intimate with natural patterns and

The sapling persists inside the older tree.

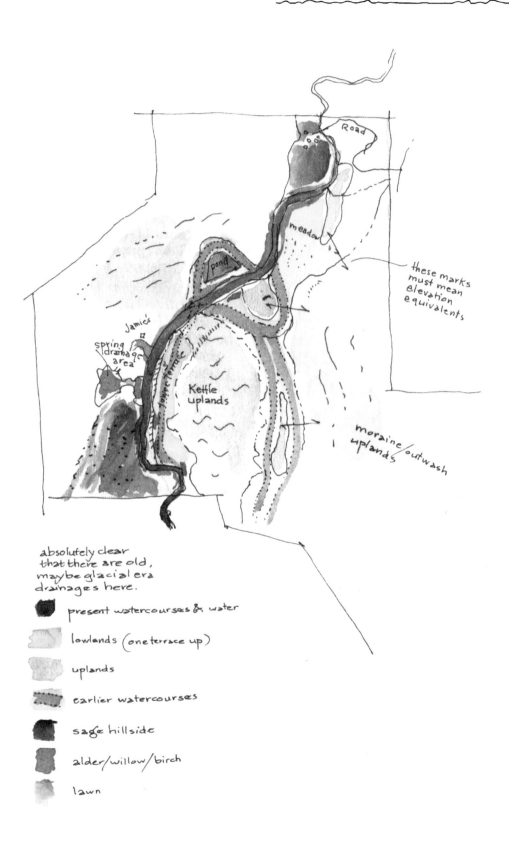

Road

meadow

these marks
must mean
elevation
equivalents

pond

Jamie's

spring
drainage
area

upper terrace

Kettle
uplands

moraine/outwash
uplands

absolutely clear
that there are old,
maybe glacial era
drainages here.

present watercourses & water

lowlands (one terrace up)

uplands

earlier watercourses

sage hillside

alder/willow/birch

lawn

cycles we can stumble onto insights about ways to live, then so much the better. The little drawing I made to help me visualize the branch-engulfing mechanism prompted plenty of other musings, such as: where is the point of most fervent growth? What species of tree best matches the pattern my life has taken? I've been slow to mature, though I sent out a lot of vigorous, flexible early growth. I'll never be a towering, dominant matriarch, like some of the rugged old white oaks whose branches are nearly as big as trunks themselves. But I'm planted in a place that suits me, where I've gained a solid roothold, and I have room to spread out.

As you ramble, observe, and record, let your attention move past what's immediately before you, to some of the design and structure questions behind the individual forms. The same principle, for instance, determines the curling of a dead leaf, the shapes of dried mud, the spiraling of a bighorn ram's horns, the shape of the human lip, and the structure of DNA. It's simply this: if the rates of growth or expansion of two surfaces is unequal, the material curls so that the slower growing surface ends up inside the faster growing surface.

The sheer variety of natural forms sometimes obscures the importance of constraints like unequal growth rates. As Lyall Watson points out in his book *Beyond Supernature*, "A flat sheet of growing cells.... is virtually compelled, when those cells in the center increase in size more rapidly than the rest, to produce a bulge. And this bulge can only grow in, like a pouch, or stick out like a thumb. And once a tissue passes any such point of decision, it is committed to a certain line of development and cannot turn back."

If you take the time to look at bubbles,

wasps nests, crystal facets, tortoise shells, scales, and buns baking in pan you see that their edges or sides tend to form three-way joins at angles of 120 degrees. That may seem mysterious, but behind it is the natural law that calls for the most efficient use of space with the minimum expenditure of energy. Both of these principles advise me when I look at and draw a tangled woodland: order out of apparent chaos.

These are the clean elegant laws of structure, the skeleton upon which the apparently meatier, messier aspects of life are hung. From ordinary observation we can begin to recognize and appre-

ciate such universal patterns, and speculate on our own about their intricacies.

We run into a different, but related field of inquiry when we consider not just the form of a snowflake, for example, but how it grows and what shapes it as it grows. The relatively new field of chaos theory looks at patterns in uncertainty, the subtle balances that rule such hard-to-define movements as weather systems and the shapes of shore-

lines, drainages, and lightning bolts. With the help of computers that can take a model and run it through billions of possible variations, we are able to get a better picture of a complex world that would have been beyond our power to "read" before.

Many people are by now familiar with an exaggerated version of one of chaos theory's earliest disclosures, nicknamed "The Butterfly Effect"—

agave plant must be lily family

the idea that a butterfly stirring the air in Peking today can transform the storm systems in New York next month. The effects predicted by the theory are actually more subtle than that, but "The Butterfly Effect" caricatures a phenomenon known as "sensitive dependence on initial conditions." In other words, tiny differences in input can become astronomical differences in output.

Chaos theorists have studied the snowflake, and developed a new model for its growth, which James Gleick, in his book *Chaos*, describes as the "very essence of chaos: a delicate balance between forces of stability and forces of instability; a powerful interplay of forces on atomic scales and forces on everyday scales." Ice crystals have an innate symmetry, and so the snowflake has a natural tendency toward the six-sided pattern we know so well. But other influences come into play during the snowflake's trip from cloud to ground, including fluctuating temperatures, how much moisture is in the air to be incorporated into the growing crystal, and the constraints of surface tension.

When an unbroken, delicately branching snow crystal lands on my sleeve, then, I can do more than just admire it or compare it to lace. I can think about how it records the history of all the weather conditions it experienced on the way down, or I can

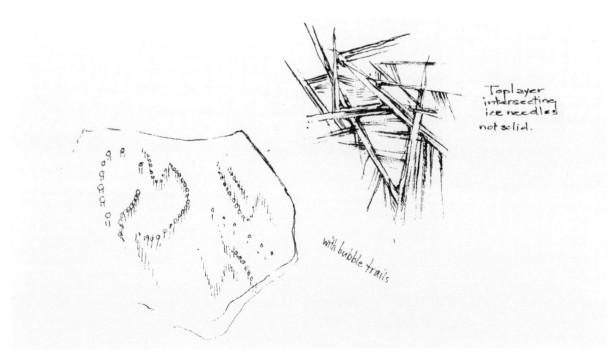

Top layer intersecting ice needles not solid.

with bubble trails

examine the individual patterns of spikes and plates that combine to form this particular crystal. I can see in it an image of the universe's tendency to organize matter into ever more elaborate configurations, countered by the forces that tend to blunt and disintegrate them. I can see it as a potent image of the self, which, no matter what vicissitudes it encounters, still keeps its integral form, and turns a setback into another kind of growth.

And not only can I focus my gaze on the snowflake in isolation, but I can see it as one among all in the air around me, covering the perennials in my garden under a variety of mounds. (Can I tell which species by the shape of the mound?) And then I can look into the distance, and see that the wall of the Absarokas are reduced to an abstract pattern of indigo cliffs, whiter tundra snowfields, and shifting veils of falling snow.

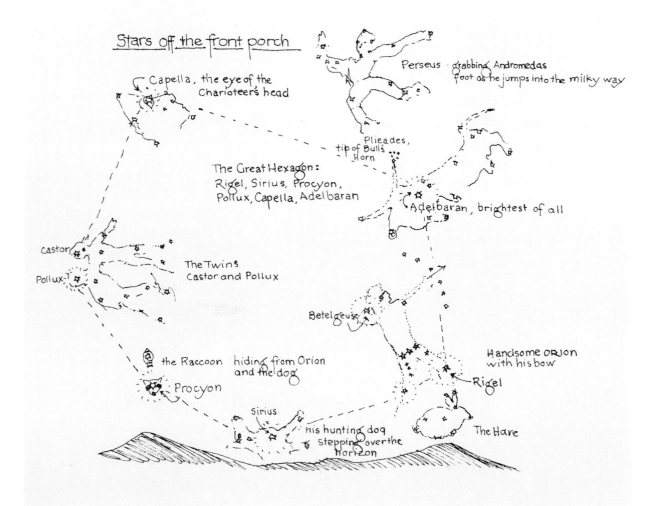

Plan one or several expeditions in which your object is to look for patterns. Spend at least half a day in a place that is either well-known to you, or typical of the local landscape where you live. Don't seek out the rarest or most enthralling corners of your home turf—because the admiration reflex might distract you from underlying structures.

Let's say you choose to visit a fairly good-size park within an urban area. You are used to following a route with your dog, so you've come to see your park as a linear journey offering a variety of vistas. Your dog amplifies the journey by his information-gathering, so you've learned to watch for other dogs, places where squirrels might be ambushed, and favorite local dog scent-kiosks. Now you are ready to layer this knowledge with other kinds, on larger and smaller scales.

Find a vantage point that affords you the widest view of the park, or the part of it most familiar to you. What's the larger landscape that this place is a slice of? Bring a topographic map, so you can study the park as a small-scale form, related to the large-scale form of the surrounding country. Make your own rough map in the journal that tries to show hills, terraces, streams, rivers, or bottom-lands. See if you can feel, by drawing, the pattern-rhythms in play where

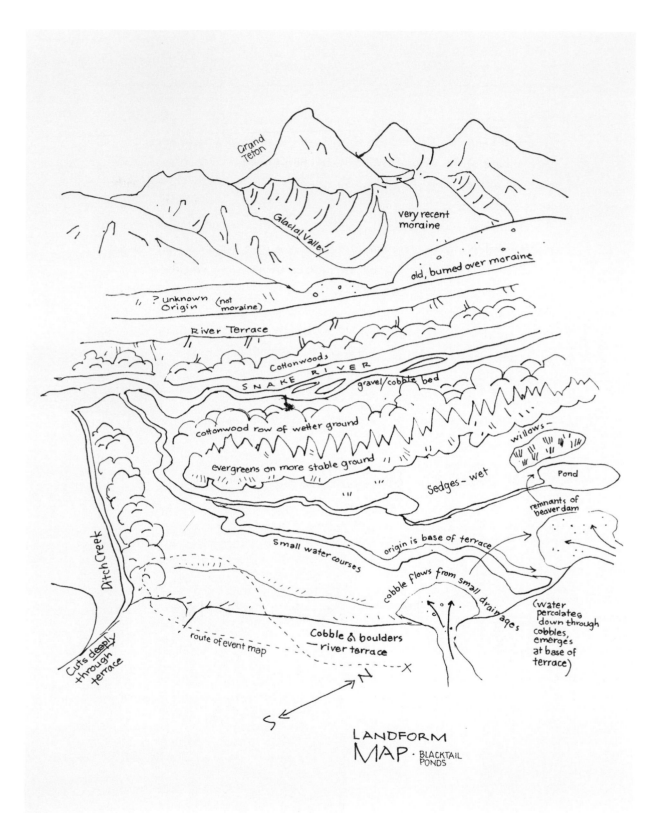

Grand Teton

Glacial Valley

very recent moraine

old, burned over moraine

? unknown Origin (not moraine)

River Terrace

Cottonwoods

S N A K E   R I V E R

gravel/cobble bed

Cottonwood row of wetter ground

evergreens on more stable ground

willows —

Pond

Sedges – wet

remnants of beaver dam

Small water courses

origin is base of terrace

Ditch Creek

cobble flows from small drainages

(water percolates down through cobbles, emerges at base of terrace)

route of event map

Cobble & boulders — river terrace

N

S

Cuts deeply through terrace

LANDFORM MAP · BLACKTAIL PONDS

116

you are. You might have to extrapolate, either because you can't see enough, or because the surrounding landforms have been obliterated by building.

Perhaps you're one of those who has a bird-like sense of direction, always aware of your orientation to the cardinal directions. If not, place yourself, either from observing the sun, or matching what you see to your map Say the park is situated on a peninsula of land bounded by two small ravines that converge with a larger creek below. As you begin to explore, bear in mind that you are walking on a peninsula, keep picturing your position on the map, and visit the edges of the ravines and the tip of the peninsula, to see how quickly it's being eroded, and to see if any bedrock is exposed where the land drops off.

Scan what's growing in the park; take a little tour looking at different kinds of vegetation in different places. Has all of it been planted? Are there places that might have been disturbed, but have grown back without interference? Are the

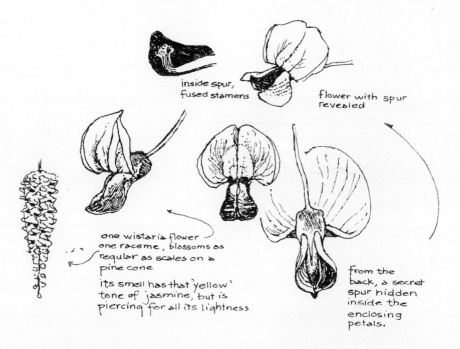

inside spur, fused stamens

flower with spur revealed

one wistaria flower
one raceme, blossoms as regular as scales on a pine cone

its smell has that 'yellow' tone of jasmine, but is piercing for all its lightness

from the back, a secret spur hidden inside the enclosing petals.

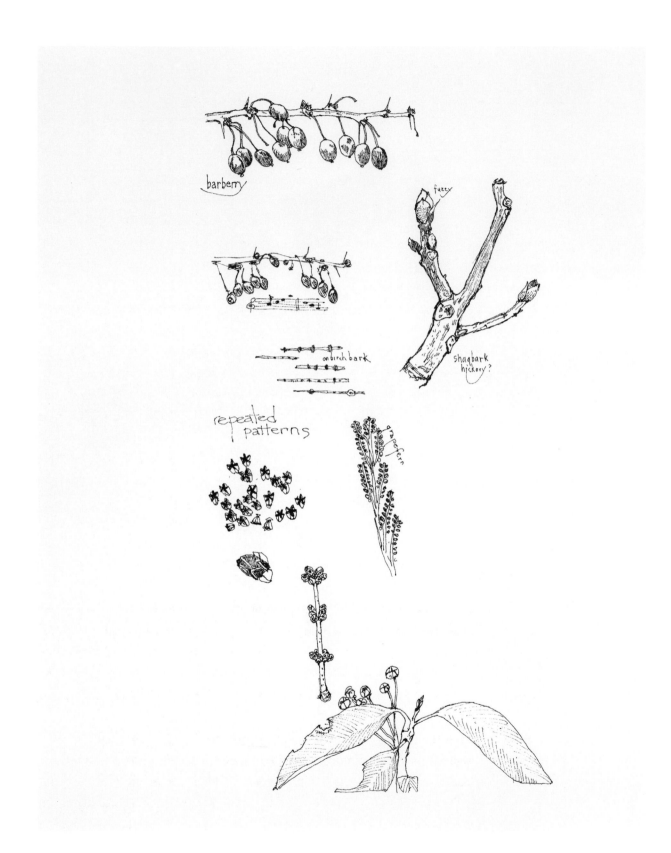

barberry

fuzzy

shagbark hickory?

on birch bark

repeated patterns

grape fern

118

trees the kinds that might be found in local native forests, if there are any? Are there any remnants of what grew here before it was a park?

Choose what you consider to be the handsomest or the most interesting tree in the area. If there are no handsome or interesting trees, settle on one that seems to be struggling, and making it. Walk slowly around this tree to understand its shape in three dimensions. Think of it as a volume. Think of the space it encloses as a body. Make a couple of very simplified drawings or diagrams that show its overall shape, devising a way to show it in three dimensions.

What's the nature of this tree's growth habit? Is it dense and twiggy, with lots of opportunistic new growth, or is it mostly big limbs now, a settled and mature tree? Do its branches droop, or does it hold them horizontally, vertically, or in a fountain shape?

Think of this tree as a three-dimensional field in which each leaf or needle is arranged to gather maximum sunlight. How is that accomplished here? Does it have an airy interior, or a dense one? If you are in a desert, you may see that this tree has ways of gathering sunlight, but avoiding dessication. How does it do that? If your tree is deciduous, take a close look at one of its leaves, and at how the veins are arranged. As the artist Paul Klee noted, "The plane form that comes into being is dependent on the interlocking lines. And where the power of the line ends, the contour, the limit of the the plane form, arises." How does the leaf in your hand illustrate that principle?

Look around on the ground until you find one or several things that came from the tree. How do these bits reflect the nature of the tree that you are coming to know? What details about how it grows can you discover from what you've found? Draw these things, slowing down and sitting still under or near the tree. As you sit and draw, keep aware of the presence of the tree. Is it moving in the wind? How does it move? Are things falling from it, are animals visiting it, nesting in it, or traveling through it? Is it giving off a fragrance, or making a sound? Make notes about these things around your drawings.

Examine the bark of your tree, as it appears on the trunk, and, if any are within reach, on the twigs. What's the growth method of the bark on the trunk?

Pleats, furrows, plates, scales, a smooth membrane? Is it vastly different from the twig bark? Where does one kind become the other? By reading the bark on the trunk, can you determine anything of this tree's history? If there are branches to look at closely, try to determine, by changes in the texture and color of the bark, which sections were last year's growth, which are this year's. A bud contains not just leaves, but a twig with several leaves, and if you look carefully you can see how much volume has been added to the tree's body over several years.

Look at the tree as a piece of architecture, as a heavy structure that has had to engineer ways to defy gravity. Where is the strength massed in the tree, where has the most reinforcement been added? Where is it most, and least, flexible?

By now, you've probably discovered that the pattern of growth is the same throughout all parts of the tree. The pattern is determined by the "way" of that particular species of tree, its order. So, the limbs on the trunk, the branches on the limb, the twigs on the branch, and the leaves on the twig will all follow the same arrangement. Even the flowers, and the reproductive parts of the flowers, will mirror the overall design, as will the fruit. But chaos, of course, has a shaping hand in the form of wind, insects, drought, diseases, lightning, people.

When the tree was a seedling and had only two branches, the loss of one bud would change its future. Has it suffered a lot of damage, can you see where limbs have broken off or been removed, or where a limb took over the job of the central trunk? If this is a tree that has seen vicissitudes, what would its ideal form look like? Its underlying growth pattern may be determined, but it isn't rigidly fixed: it can compensate for its mishaps. How has this one compensated?

As you walk away from your tree, watch how its appearance alters as it recedes in the distance. Would you recognize it on the streets of Paris?

Later, when you are in a reflective frame of mind, begin a diagram of your life as a tree-form, using your exploration of the tree in the park as a metaphorical model.

d

x 2

a. Ubiquitous bronze green beetle, related to June Bugs, much eaten by bluebirds (we watched them) and maybe by bats because their guano is so beetle-wing shiny

b Sedge, that is as thick as turf on stream banks.

c. One of many severely shorn willows, now managing to put out more shoots, being chewed up by things, and rolled-up-and-bound by such as this tiny caterpillar.

d. The dominant emergent — this one has a very wiggly sexy hula-action abdomen

e. What I called "Henbit" but what somebody else called "Self-heal"

f. Blue-eyed grass, but it really has a bright yellow eye

c.

b

PLANAR SURFACES

REPEATED GESTURES: BEECH TWIGS

FERN FRONDS SPRING FROM A CIRCULAR BASE

Chapter 7

UNMEASURABLE PHENOMENA

Out in the irrigated hay meadows in June, the grasses are dense, arched and swaying, the perfect emblem of summer. I watch them bowing in clumps, and run their intricately fringed heads through my fingers. They change color as they rise and fall in a fresh wind. Seeing them makes me think of a passage in Thoreau's journal, where he refers to the "washing days" of June. I kneel down to scrawl a note reminding myself to look up the phrase when I get home; meanwhile an assortment of leaf-hoppers rains down on the open book.

A copy of *Walden* sits on the shelf next to Thoreau's journals, and though I reread it every decade or so, and admire it, I much prefer his daily, wide-ranging investigations to *Walden*'s high moral tone. That sometimes pontifical voice reveals the side of him that is prissy and suspicious, maidenly—a person who doesn't trust the physical, and suspects that nature, underneath her beauty, is vul-

gar. I know he'd be one of those men who would bring out the brazen strumpet in me. I'd want to shake him into embracing sensuality, and convince him that a comely shrub oak is no substitute for the mysterious abyss of womanhood. And I'd buy him a good pen and some decent paper.

His fourth volume, May 1852 to February 1853, is a good place to start looking for his reference to "washing days," since this kind of description probably comes from his middle years. By 1852 he no longer felt compelled to interpret everything through the classics, but he hadn't yet subsided into naturalist's shorthand of lists and dates. I skip over the detailed descriptions of plants and animals, comparisons of sightings and bloom times, to search out his general remarks on the season, his attempts to define just what distinguishes the end of May from the beginning of June.

"Now is the season of the leafing of trees and

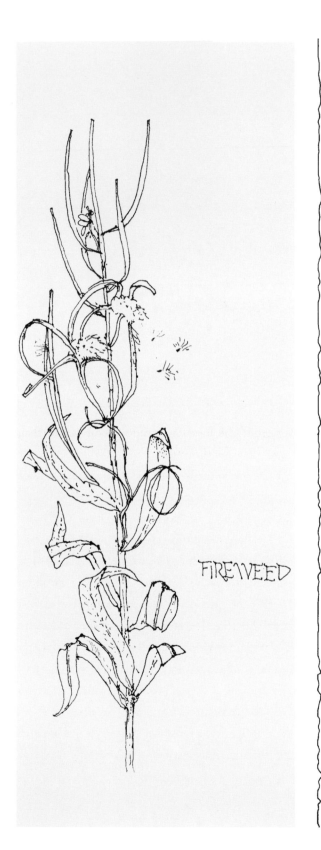

FIREWEED

of planting," he writes. ".... Perchance the beginning of summer may be dated from the fully formed leaves when dense shade (?) begins. I will see." And this: "The prospect from these rocks is early-June-like. You notice the tender light green of the birches, both white and paper, and the brown-red tops of the maples where their keys are."

I cross the room to the glass-fronted bookcase and find a volume of my own journals that records a similar moment. One morning thirteen years ago, looking across a lake at a Connecticut hillside in April, I realized that each species of tree can be known by its leafing-out or flowering colors. I'd noted a shade of red that morning, too, which turned out to be not maple keys in this case, but their blossoms. A few pages later I sketched branches of six species of trees, realizing that the way each extends its new season's growth is also characteristic: "Beech droops. Ash extends symmetrically. Maple makes pagodas. Oak like small mice. Horse-chestnut umbrellas. Pignut hickory like cupped hands."

Returning to Thoreau, I find this entry for May 30: "Now is the summer come. A breezy, washing day. A day for shadows, even of moving clouds, over fields in which the grass is beginning to wave."

On June 9 he expands on it: "For a week past we have had *washing* days. The grass waving, and trees having leaved out, their boughs wave and feel the effect of the breeze. Thus new life and motion is imparted to the trees. This is the first half of June. The general leafiness, shadiness, and waving of grass and boughs in the breeze characterize the season."

Then on June 23, apparently still mulling this over, he writes: "It is what I call a *washing* day.... an agreeably cool and clear and breezy day, when all

things appear as if washed bright and shine, and, at this season especially, the sound of the wind rustling the leaves is like the rippling of a stream, and you see the light-colored underside of the still fresh foliage, and a sheeny light is reflected from the bent grass in the meadows."

Seeing these entries strung together, I find his persistence endearing, as he adds to his first impression, polishes it, makes it more specific. It must be something like the delight of not only *looking* at the inviting surface of Walden Pond, but plunging into it. In finding words that marry experience and response, he knows the deepest pleasure of the writer. Without the words, he's looking at the surface; in finding the words he immerses himself. He keeps refining the idea of "washing days" to get closer to the truth. It isn't just an apt phrase tossed off as a writerly coup. And there's the effect on the reader: his words have made me feel the per-

fection of the June hay meadow more keenly than I could have without them.

He moves easily between the perceptions of artist and naturalist, without a hint of apology. Since his day, both science and art have become more entrenched in their own conventions; Thoreau seems to have no self-consciousness about joining their forces. It requires the predisposition of an artist to search out and pay attention to combinations of atmosphere, color, and form. The trained naturalist of today would be unlikely to focus on such nebulous features: they can't be measured, and the resulting discoveries won't add to any established body of knowledge.

Consider some of the other subjects that came under Thoreau's scrutiny in Volume 4:

- shapes of clouds and how they move

- the way wind reveals itself moving across water

styles
of grasses

126

- how the surface of water reflects light in different ways

- how cloud shadows affect the view of a landscape

- how dew forms on leaves according to their different textures

- the sources of different fragrances encountered during a walk

- ice forms created by the splashing of water over rocks (with half a dozen sketches)

- whether sounds in the night are of insect, bird, or amphibian origin

Thoreau, with his insatiable appetite for phenomena, relished and reported on the unmeasurable as well as the measurable. The twentieth century has produced no scientific literature about the way light and wind work on the surface of a pond, for instance, unless the adherents of chaos theory are at work on it. There are no papers published about it, no seminars, no grants given to study it. And because no named category exists for that and similar phenomena, most of us don't see them.

Of course, with enough effort and the help of powerful computers, we could measure and name these events, digesting them into formulae. But would that be their best interpretation? I doubt that ice-forms along moving water have ever been studied with such devotion as Thoreau gave them. In his entry of January 26, 1853, he wrote, "The coarse spray had frozen as it fell on the rocks, and formed shell-like crusts over them, with irregular but beautifully clear and sparkling surfaces like egg-shaped diamonds, each being the top of a club-shaped and branched fungus icicle." And then he drew them. Any attempt to quantify that kind

7:00 No clouds. 43°

CLOUD LOG
JULY 8

10:30

windless
cirrus floccus? Just a few

11:30

windless

getting very hot—
what began as flattened
"altocumulus floccus"
has now built up— covering 50%
of sky...

12:00

Developing bases on
these cumulus "humilus" and "mediocris"
developing in certain areas below the "floccus"

one's beginning
to get that "towering"
look

128

12:30

This congestus
has towered &
been blown over
by winds aloft

Now the "altocumulus floccus" are <u>dissolving</u>
and the cumulus "humilus" & "mediocritus" are becoming, RAPIDLY
"CUMULUS CONGESTUS." I would say with about 90% certainty
that we'll hear thunder by dinner.   Wind 9 mph

1:00

The same
big one as
above is now
producing thunder
and rain....

"Congestus" hardly says it: these cells are piling up, coalescing.
Pieces of scud are breaking off & turning into ice crystal filaments
at high altitude — others are little gray rogues at lower levels

2:00

Towards the east
the congestus seem to form & move in rows.
Towards the west they seem much bigger, more unstable
collapsing downward into rain or upward into ice clouds.
Wind increases — gusts of 15-20 mph alternates hot & cool.

129

cloud log 4:30 Valley-wide thunderstorm!! 67°

of observation, it seems to me, would prove less fruitful than his direct description, employing both words and imagery.

A journal-keeper can produce pages of intriguing drawings and dead-on descriptions of cloud shapes and sky changes in the span of one summer day, and find a way to organize them that suits the material. My students have proven that to me in the form of "cloud logs," updated hourly, from dawn to nightfall. We learn the names of different kinds of clouds as the hours pass and new ones appear, consulting cloud charts and field guides to the atmosphere. But simply listing them doesn't satisfy us, we want to know them more fully, to understand the reasons for their day-long transformations, to draw them and trace their shapes. And we want language as vivid as Thoreau's, to contain the excitement of our discoveries, to partake of their sensuous nature.

When Thoreau notes the brown-red of the maples in his "June-like" landscape, his starting point is a painterly response, an overall appreciation for the subtle palette of colors before him. A botanist would see the mix and distribution of species, a geologist would look for signs of glaciation, or the shape of the underlying landform, a birder would be watching and listening for birds; I'm sure Thoreau was doing all three and more. But his special gift is the breadth of his curiosity, the fact that it includes so many categories, and, more telling, that it sees past, or between categories. "Colors of Trees at a Distance, in Different Seasons" is not a subject I've seen treated in detail, but Thoreau would be able to write the book on it, creating both an informed field guide and an inspired literary work.

Since art and science have equal attraction for me, my journals are full of accounts of unmeasurable phenomena. One specialty is "kinds of shadows cast on the bottoms of shallow streams by the movement of the water surface, or things floating on it." There isn't much competition in my field so far.

Developing an eye for unmeasurable phenomena usually begins, like most creative endeavors, with a period of apparent inattention, or diffuse attention. Diffuse attention is inclusive, it monitors the whole moment, but for we who are accustomed to focused attention, it is hard to indulge. Most of us have learned at least to be on the alert for beauty, but even that sensitivity can make us miss much, since beauty has been fairly rigidly defined in our culture. For instance, the predilection for "grand" scenery or "peaceful" countryside can be a limitation, because selecting grandeur or peacefulness will mean we won't see the dung beetle take possession of the final dropping from a freshly road-killed ground squirrel. If I had looked at the trees on the Connecticut hillside as only pretty, I wouldn't have troubled to go a little deeper, to discover that I could tell beech from oak from red maple that early in the season.

The closest thing to a catch-all discipline for unmeasurable phenomena would probably be phenology, "the study of natural phenomena that recur periodically, as migration, blossoming, etc., and of their relation to climate and changes in season." This, along with principles of ecology and natural selection, were Thoreau's ruling scientific passions, and there is no reason to think that his collection of ice observations couldn't, with a little stretch of the definition, be considered a form of phenology. So could the cloud logs. It would require that we include non-living things in the category of "phenomena that recur periodically."

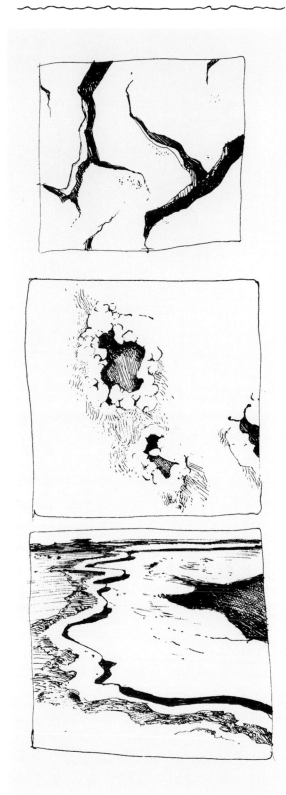

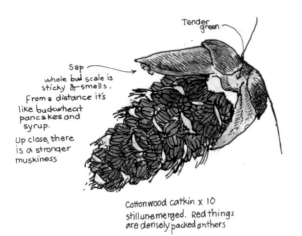

Tender green

Sap

whole bud scale is sticky & smells.
From a distance it's like buckwheat pancakes and syrup.

Up close, there is a stronger muskiness

Cottonwood catkin x 10
still unemerged. Red things are densely packed anthers

New spruce growth extending, carrying papery bud scales

And this branch of the discipline would urge minute observation and description of the subject, in addition to noting its periodicity.

Anyone who has had occasion to use the Peterson's *Field Guide to Rocky Mountain Wildflowers*, written by John and Frank Craighead, will know about the comments under "flowering season" that say, "When the dogtooth violet begins to flower, mating calls of saw-whet owls can be heard and mule deer are beginning to fawn. At 8000 to 9000 feet, height of flowering season is early July, when white-tailed ptarmigan, gray-crowned rosy finch and water pipit are nesting." A more recent book of Frank Craighead's, *For Everything There is a Season*, views the whole Greater Yellowstone Ecosystem through the lens of phenology. Thoreau's oft-repeated phrase "It is the season of... " finds a refrain in Craighead's "Now is when the.... "

Journal-keepers, because they are creating a life-long record of their encounters, are natural phe-

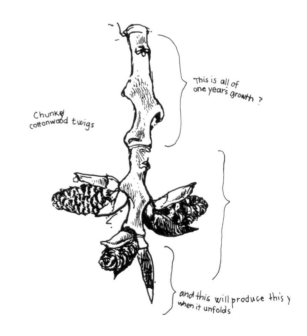

This is all of one year's growth ?

Chunky cottonwood twigs

and this will produce this y when it unfolds

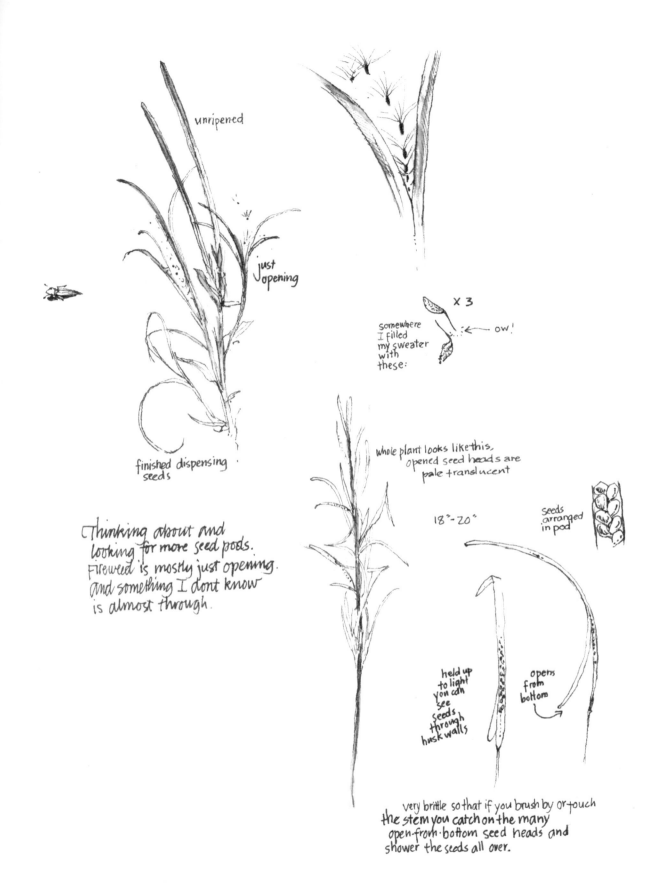

unripened

just opening

finished dispensing seeds

X 3

somewhere I filled my sweater with these: ← ow!

Thinking about and looking for more seed pods. Fireweed is mostly just opening. and something I dont know is almost through.

whole plant looks like this, opened seed heads are pale translucent

18"-20"

seeds arranged in pod

held up to light you can see seeds through husk walls

opens from bottom

very brittle so that if you brush by or touch the stem you catch on the many open-from-bottom seed heads and shower the seeds all over.

In the aspen grove for
an hour or so drawing
& experiencing.

Piles of gold coin leaves
and more falling with
each gust

Sky the particular violet-
blue it becomes when
juxtaposed with yelloworange.

Or else deep blue black gray,
undersides of sept. clouds

Ponies gnawing aspen bark —
listening to creaking branches

Michael taking pictures
of leaves

September gusts and
sharp light & shadow changing

Fine ride — loathe to return

Aspen leaves blowing & falling

Wind Rivers in distance

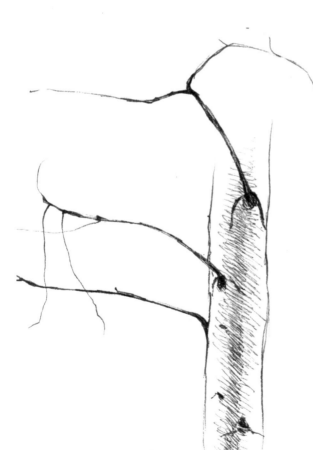

nologists. The habit of granting each day its singularity lays the groundwork for seeing into the hidden seasons, and seasons-within-seasons. The seasons, and thousands of other things that move us, reveal themselves in unmeasurable phenomena, like Thoreau's "sheeny light" on the bent grass in the meadows.

To capture the unmeasurable, first you must learn to notice it. Then you must invent ways to show light, shapes, sequences, processes, patterns, and the passage of time—not to mention colors, sounds, geometries, pathways, interactions and metamorphoses. To me, this realm is the richest of all for journal-keepers, a territory that hasn't been given its due. To record it properly requires the best of the artist, poet, and observer, a supple blending of inquiry and receptivity.

The number-scientists will continue to graph their data, preferring to chart only the measurable world. That leaves the field wide open for Thoreauvian journal-keepers and other alert mavericks to plumb the unmeasurable.

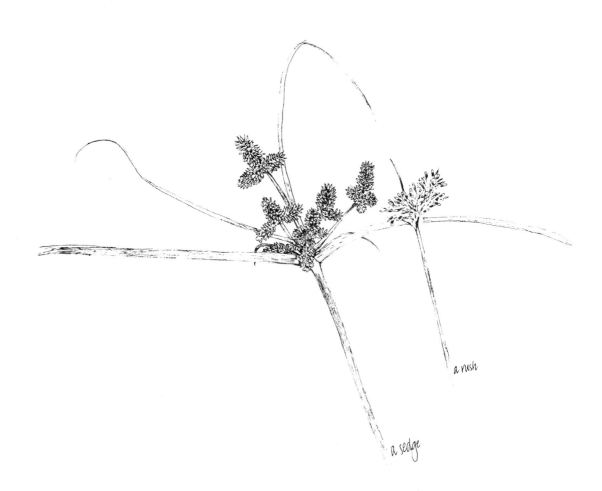

a rush

a sedge

August 24 · 1994

Letter
to
Thoreau

Dear Henry ———

August has followed a pattern
similar to the one you described: a
shift from hot, blazing dog days to a
distinctly autumnal feel — a wall
of thunderstorms two days ago
ushered in the change, but of course
it was there in the angle of light, and
in the plants which are finishing their
work for the year, before the air
concurred.

I've walked up to squirrel Hill this
morning, and a little beyond — needed
to be outside right away on this
beautifully poised hour & season—
not actively fall yet, but summer's
forward motion has ceased. Like
a weight on a long string, the year
is wound up tight in spring & then
released, to unwind and with its own
momentum, wind itself up again—
now it's at that still point between
winding & unwinding

daddy
longlegs

alder

parsnip
leaves?

no....
water
hemlock...

wound up tight
stored energy

end of
winter,
poised

expending energy
spring/summer

wrapping up
again,
storing
energy
summer/fall

Goes through another unwrap,
rewrap cycle through the winter,
winter solstice being bottom of
the curve ....

This hill, I guess it's called Lobo
Hill, is a mixture of meadow &
forest, little ravines, gentle ridges.
There are many Douglas fir, and
so a host of nutcrackers and
red squirrels. As usual, there are
patriarch firs or groups of them,
that tower over the bulk of younger
forest, and that's where the squirrels
seem to be doing their most
concentrated work. There's an
agitated character up in the top,
cone-bearing part of one big tree —

Weather is the perfect natural phenomena for the scrutiny of the journal-keeper. It's always happening, you don't have to go far to check on it, and you need no sophisticated equipment to study it. You may want to collect weather observations in one place in your journal, in the form of a weather log that covers a month or a season. Allow yourself lots of room, because drawings, even paintings, and other kinds of graphic interpretations will figure heavily in it.

If you want to keep track of the year's lurching progress toward spring, a graph will prove useful. Graphs don't have to be dry compilations stripped of grace and invention; they can be a perfect way to blend art and information. You might do a strip diagram, using areas of different tone and texture to illustrate the pattern of cloudy and clear days, perhaps even tying it visually to the temperature graph. These could be the basic framework of a weather log.

But I'm envisioning here a more inclusive kind of weather observation, one that tries to penetrate and describe some of the less obvious facets of weather. How is the day acting, what's its humor? How is it affecting animals, plants, and people? What kinds of clouds appear during the day (you can name them yourself, or become acquainted with the typical varieties through one of the excellent field guides). How are they acting? How quickly are they changing? What do they seem to indicate?

Even after years of jet travel, a shocking number of people still walk around seeing clouds as flat cutouts on a flat sky. Draw the various clouds and cloud formations you see, paying particular attention to their volumes in space, their lights and shadows. Most clouds form at a particular altitude and ride on that air layer, as with cumulus clouds whose tops sometimes mount into higher zones, or certain cirrus clouds that send streamers into the strata below. There might be several layers of clouds stacked up in the sky at once. Cloud shapes are abstract and hard to define. Drawing them will teach you about the wordless physical language of natural forms.

Try to learn about the way big weather patterns work in your area, and speculate on how your vista of sky demonstrates what's going on in the whole region. Weather books, with the help of computer imaging, are getting better and better at showing the three-dimensional shapes of large-scale systems. I was never able to understand the physics of low and high pressure ridges and troughs by looking at the old, two-dimensional, symbol-filled charts. Now, from having pondered the latest illustrations, which are in turn informed by the marvel of satellite images, I think I understand their invisible shapes. I keep hoping that the Weather Channel will evolve into the feast for the weather-hungry that it could be: so far it's still too stingy with those time-lapse satellite clips to satisfy me.

Once you begin to investigate the weather, you'll be pulled outdoors by all kinds of curiosities, as I am about to be this minute. From the corral gate, I can see a few medium-height clouds that have been shredded into filaments by a high wind aloft. But what called me out is a perfect row of little cottonball clouds, whose top surfaces are also being shredded. Are they what's left of a single larger cloud, broken by turbulence into almost identical pieces?

Now the tops are not just shredding, but being molded into lens-shaped tiers. I know what the "lenticular" look means: there is a "mountain wave" effect occurring here behind the mass of the Wind River Range. Similar conditions produce the row of waves behind a boulder as water flows over it.

So my air turbulence theory is a fairly plausible way to explain the row of clouds. The entire weather pattern is changing right at this moment, from a frigid arctic high to a chinook-driven thaw. Without having to look at the rest of the clouds, I'd bet that they are all changing into lenticular forms.

Watching weather is a good way to begin distinguishing the seasons-within-seasons that so intrigued Thoreau. As you learn to make ever finer distinctions among conditions, and match those up with the angle of the light, and changes in the landscape, sub-seasons will make themselves known to you. If you think you've identified one, make a special note of it in the log, and give it a name. Next year, review your earlier logs and watch to see if the same configuration appears again.

1.   Waterstriders
make four sets
of ripple marks
w/each stroke

2.   shadow cast on
bottom shows
shadows for each
surface tension
dimple

3.   Bubbles get
carried intact
far down stream
from riffles

4.   Water glitters like
aspen leaves
going over riffles

5.   Water bending
but not breaking
reflection

6.   Small between-
rock-puddles,
where snails
trundle

W H A T   W A T E R   D O E S

139

You might find yourself getting so caught up in the clouds that you undertake the study of meteorology; soon you'll be musing over adiabatic lapse-rate equations when you look skyward. You may become so engaged that you start designing experiments to try to prove your theories. But even without the equations, tests, and proofs, you are still doing science, at the theoretical and speculative end of the spectrum.

In temperate regions, before spring gets going, select a half dozen different species of shrubs: willows, alders, roses, junipers, forsythia, raspberries, etc., or young trees, as long as they have twigs at eye level. Study their winter shapes and colors, draw or diagram them. Visit them regularly, and make records of the changes you see as spring progresses.

All these plants not only have different leaf shapes, but each has a unique way of packing the leaves inside the bud, breaking the bud sheath, unfurling the leaves, and extending the shoot. And what about catkins, cones, and flowers? Male or female? What transitions do they go through? Drawing and comparing are the best ways to learn about this annual extravaganza. That doesn't mean that

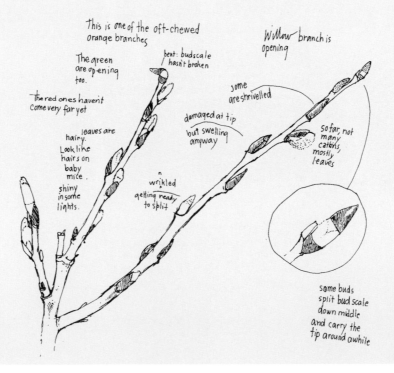

you can't introduce a formal layout for this exercise: drawings in a grid, showing each twig at each stage of development, reading horizontally or vertically, might reveal similarities and differences better than a random page-spread of drawings, in this case.

Attend first to the overall shapes and how they reveal processes, rather than being diverted by details of color and texture or light and shadow. Visual editing, being able to select the most important elements, is essential in drawing. Without it, you are likely to lose the thread of your original excitement, and equally likely to get bogged down in a drawing that tries to do everything at once.

In the fall, when you're sure it's no longer in use, search out a bird's nest and bring it home with you. If it's attached to a minor branch of a tree, so that the tree won't be damaged by its removal, bring branch and nest intact. Draw it and examine it as a piece of structural engineering, first as a whole, then take it apart to see if you can determine the sequence in which it was built, the range of materials used in it, and the way the bird constructed it. *A Field Guide to Birds' Nests* will help you find out who built it, if you want to know that.

Birds are fussy about their building materials, often flying far to find a particular species of moss for the lining, or strips of bark from certain trees. The nest is not just a random accumulation, but represents a series of choices. And materials are used in different ways: some make up the framework, some are used to shape a container, some are provided for the warmth and comfort of the nestlings. (Be aware that if there hasn't been a hard freeze you may run into some bird parasites, as in mites or lice. I've never found them to be too annoying, but if the nest seems to be infested, work outdoors, or find a new nest.)

Spend a day along a river, creek, lake, or ocean, and make a "field guide to what water does." It might include several different varieties of reflection, foam and bubbles, flow patterns and turbulence, transparency/opacity, waves and ripples, and many, many other things. Be alert for tiny phenomena as well as great.

And of course, get acquainted with Thoreau, at his best, in his journals, and carry on his study of the unmeasurable.

Chapter 8

THE WORLD AS EVENTS

I've walked hard to reach the red sandstone head-wall of Sheep Leap Draw in the badlands, watching mostly the faint trail ahead, noting only an occasional rock wren jingle or the cuneiform jab of a deer print. If I want to continue in this vein of aerobic ground-covering, I'll have to find a route up the broken rock faces and continue my trek on the mesa. If I were up there, I could see what the weather is doing in Yellowstone. This hunger to cover ground, gain a prominence, infects everyone who walks in Wyoming.

I'd rather get in touch with the day. My body is awake, but I missed nearly everything on the way up; only the most minimal bits of information pierced my exercise consciousness. I need to stop and watch for a while. It's impossible to catch the drift of things immediately. It takes time to become present. Here's a circular toupee of (relatively) soft buffalo grass, a sign that I am supposed to sit down.

I look and listen outward in a slow arc from the near landscape, of grass and scrappy little flowers, across striped badlands battlements, to the farthest horizon, snowy peaks, then back to the near. Because my skin is still damp and air-current sensitive, its capacity as sense-organ is heightened. I note that the breezes in the canyon are fitful and vary from hot to suddenly cool, a signal that the air is unstable; active forenoon clouds rearing over the western wall of the canyon confirm that. I need to pay attention: unstable air equals aggressive thunderstorms.

Sheep Leap Canyon in its lower length is narrow and sinuous, shaded by junipers. It's one of my favorite places because its mouth, where it joins the much wider Byrd Draw, is almost invisible, obscured by brush and a couple of chunks of fallen cliff. There are never many people in the badlands, but the occasional hiker would be likely to miss this side canyon. At its head, it rounds out into a bowl.

Once there must have been a period of stasis when the canyon filled with sediment, because there is a head-high shelf of soil on which most of the junipers grow. Where the shelf is wide enough, the junipers form a little forest. Within the life-span of the junipers (some of which are hundreds of years old) the land must have lifted a bit; I see evidence that the wash is actively downcutting. A number of fine old trees have begun to lean out over the channel as the earth under their roots is washed away. Eventually they will let go, though the entire bank will have to disappear beneath them before they do. So a hoary old juniper's precarious position might take another fifty years to resolve itself.

A swift motion at the edge of my vision registers as a bird that has come to perch on one of the stone pinnacles down-canyon. I locate it, then sort through a range of possibilities for what it might be, taking into account its size and shape, how it acts, etc. A songbird might choose a perch like that, but it would be more likely to flutter up to it than swoop down on it, as this one did. This bird is the size of a robin, and also flicks its tail regularly. It has strong shoulders, much bulkier than a robin's. Now I know: it's a kestrel, the smallest falcon. I keep watching; identification is not the only objective. This falcon seems to be crouching more than usual, and craning its neck over its shoulder. What is it doing?

The day's tendrils have penetrated me now. What was static landscape has changed subtly, to a drama involving cloud and bird; both have become active agents. What are they doing? What's going on? Childishly simple questions, but they mark the trail out of separation to engagement, and to a whole world of knowledge beyond simply noting what's here, calling it beautiful, and

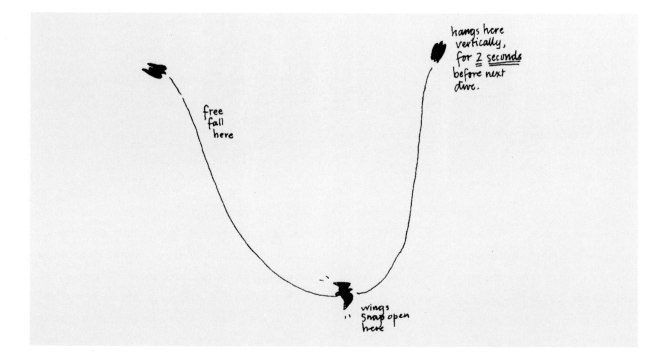

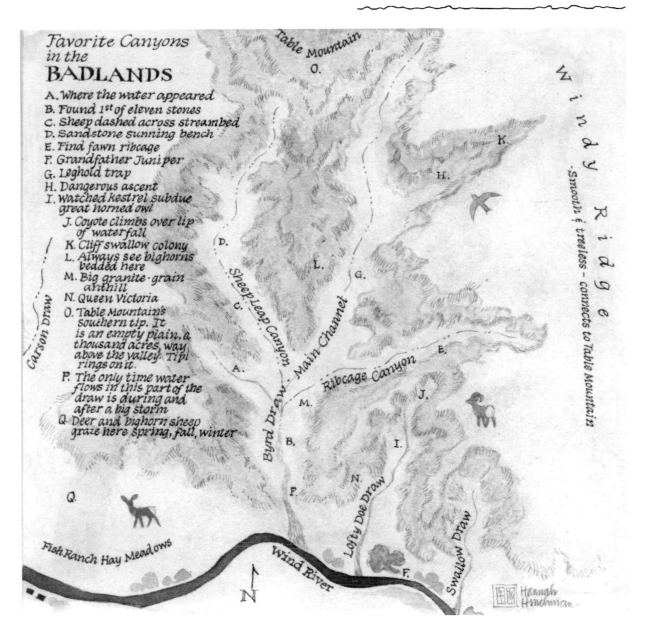

Favorite Canyons in the
BADLANDS

A. Where the water appeared
B. Found 1st of eleven stones
C. Sheep dashed across streambed
D. Sandstone sunning bench
E. Find fawn ribcage
F. Grandfather Juniper
G. Leghold trap
H. Dangerous ascent
I. Watched kestrel subdue great horned owl
J. Coyote climbs over lip of waterfall
K. Cliff swallow colony
L. Always see bighorns bedded here
M. Big granite-grain anthill
N. Queen Victoria
O. Table Mountain's southern tip. It is an empty plain, a thousand acres, way above the valley. Tipi rings on it.
P. The only time water flows in this part of the draw is during and after a big storm
Q. Deer and bighorn sheep graze here spring, fall, winter

going back to thinking about "real" life: work, money, love, family.

Above the falcon on the pinnacle, I'm able to pick out a black dot in the sky. Through binoculars I see it hover, then inscribe a wide fluttering circle, wings held downward in a stiff vee, approaching the falcon on the rock. By the show-off look of this maneuver, I guess that I'm witnessing a series of actions related to courtship, and decide to make notes in the journal so that I don't miss anything in the sequence.

My notes take the form of quick squibs of lines, alternating with descriptive words, an attempt to capture shapes, sounds and paths of

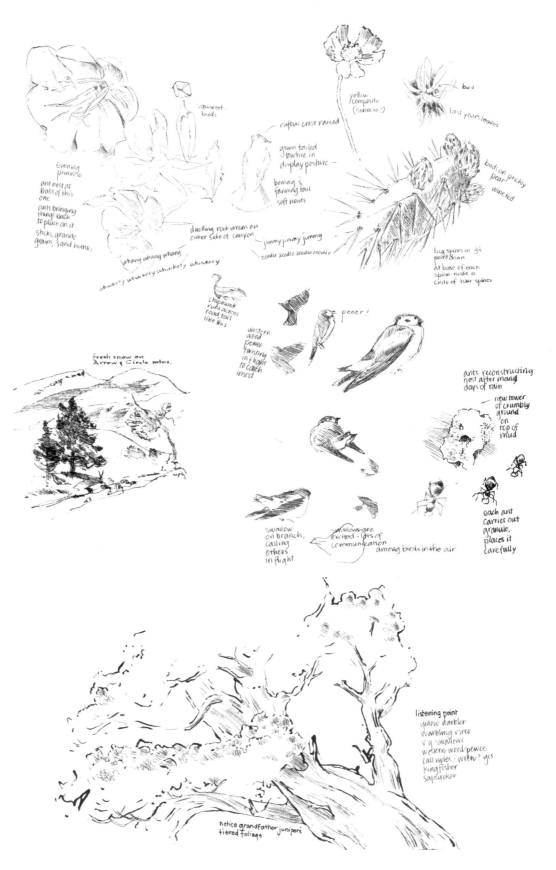

movement. The bird in flight is calling, a particular, plaintive kind of kestrel voice. The bird on the rock is calling back, more softly. The sky bird joins the ground bird, they mate in a storm of wings, then rest beside one another, facing in the same direction, each ruffling and smoothing its feathers with an air of contentment.

The day, which has up till now been a pretty background for feeling healthy, a generic day in early summer, becomes marked and separated by the event of the kestrels. And by the fact that I participated in the event by making shapes on a page in response to it.

Back home that night I go to the bookcase to pull out the volumes of Bent's *Life Histories of Birds of North America* that deal with birds of prey. Under kestrel I find this account, from William Brewster in 1925: "Today I saw them sitting not far apart on the tops of neighboring dead balsams. Every now and then one, always the male, I thought, would mount high in the air to fly very rapidly, in a wide circle over and around where the other was perched, bending the tips of his wings downward and quivering them incessantly, at the same time uttering a shrill, clamorous cry, oft repeated."

Bent's *Life Histories* is never far from my hands after walks; it's a series of volumes about birds that reflect a nineteenth-century fondness for teaching by anecdote and narrative rather than by tables and statistics. Its pages are full of personal observation, of both typical and exceptional bird behavior. The reports are always attributed to someone from the army of watchers with whom Arthur Cleveland Bent seems to have corresponded. This is a way of gathering knowledge that I like: the watchers asked, "What's going on?" and were willing to attempt an answer, based on their own powers of observation, and to record their accounts in great detail.

The questions asked more often these days are "How many? With what frequency?" I wonder whether we are alienating some of our most alert potential scientists by insisting that inquiry be car-

easter daisy

what's happening out in the sagebrush

phlox

ried out mainly by sampling and measuring, deemphasizing imagination, that most valuable "what if... " that generates theories.

The great evolutionary biologist E. O. Wilson admits in his memoir that he has no head for numbers, but rather works from a base of curiosity, rigorous observation, and well-informed speculation. He has been wise enough to enlist mathematicians to carry out many of the necessary quantitative proofs for his hypotheses. An alert naturalist, an ordinary person, is still capable of penetrating the world of appearances in a valuable way, especially if he learns to be on the watch for events, and follows through with his own research, however informal. Thoreau, today, would be dismayed to see how far intelligent observation has been shouldered out of the arena of science.

Lay people drawn to science, or at least to natural history, can and should proclaim that the world of natural phenomena is not just the domain of the researcher, the trained biologist; that any of us, if we are willing to go looking, can ask valid questions and find useful answers.

Rediscovering something that has already been

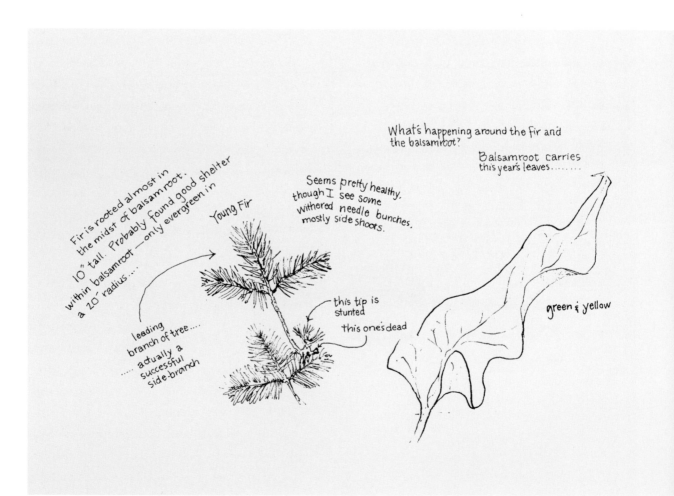

documented doesn't diminish my sense of its newness: the event of mating kestrels is new each time it's repeated, each time it issues from the source of the present.

That's why I keep returning to the word "event," though it isn't the perfect term for what I'm referring to. It implies that things happen exclusively in the form of stories, a linear cause-and-effect sequence. But this comment by Alan Watts, the late writer and Zen scholar, illuminates another, more timeless aspect of event-centered perception. "Going indoors I find that all the

major discovery

last year's leaves.....

and year before last year's leaves..

pale cocoa

silvery-gray, fragile

household furniture is alive. Everything gestures. Tables are tabling, pots are potting, walls are walling, fixtures are fixturing—a world of events instead of things."

What I think Watts means is that the intrinsic nature of things, maintaining and preserving their forms through time, is an event in itself. So, when I focus on a smooth yellow stone in the wash, linger to learn its shape, the shadow it casts, its texture, its position in the dry rivulet, it gestures through my senses. It's so distinct that it appears to be kin to a living thing, with an intention to display its own distinctive self. The moment I spend with it is a doubly lit event: the stone *is*, on its own, and it also becomes part of my apprehending mind.

Same with the gesture of the cottonwood twig back down the canyon, developing its fluff-launched seeds. Its statement is clear and adamant, inimitably cottonwood in all of its features. Alan Watts, again: "The bud has opened and the fresh leaves fan out and curve back with a gesture which is unmistakably communicative but does not say anything except, 'Thus!' And somehow that is quite satisfactory, even startlingly clear."

So, things simply "being themselves" can constitute an event, if we are awake to them. They are among the everyday miracles we have nearly ceased to see. A slight perceptual shift transforms the inert to the animate, invests the simplest situations with drama, or comedy, or a more coherent order.

If you weren't prepared for a world of events, would you be able to notice the impressive diversity of the little overgrown meadow you pass every day on the way to work? Without having first recognized its weedy health, you would probably miss, later in the summer, the moment when this-

Lavender tulips expiring
an extravagant gesture

tle and goldfinch play out their finest seasonal moment. The meadow is haloed with ripe thistle-down seed-heads, which are being defrocked by flocks of goldfinches. Thistle seeds are their favorite food, and they prefer the down over any other material to line their nests.

And yet one can't force "event perception." A keen gaze can be too exclusive, overfocused. I try to watch in an unconstructed way, allowing my attention to range from the tiniest spittle-bug in its foam house, to the hue of the weather; from the tunnel of a vole, to the way water seeps out at the edge of a shale layer. I try to keep in mind that everything I see is a clue, a detail in an as-yet untold story. Some of these are best noted as sketches, some as paragraphs, some as diagrams,

some as maps, some as full-fledged drawings. And there are times when to insert the journal would be to impose on the flow of events—better to watch, commit to memory, and create the account later.

The idea of encouraging event perception occurred as I noticed, in my teaching, that would-be naturalist/journal-keepers are *prevented* from seeing the natural world. They are prevented first by categories: if no perceptual path exists for recognizing a swallow, they won't see one (they will see the undifferentiated "bird," instead). And they are prevented, second, by the habit of seeing the world as dead. An unawakened watcher set down in the midst of nature sees it flatly, as an inert, unliving "scene," rather than as the seething of life, movement, transformation that it is.

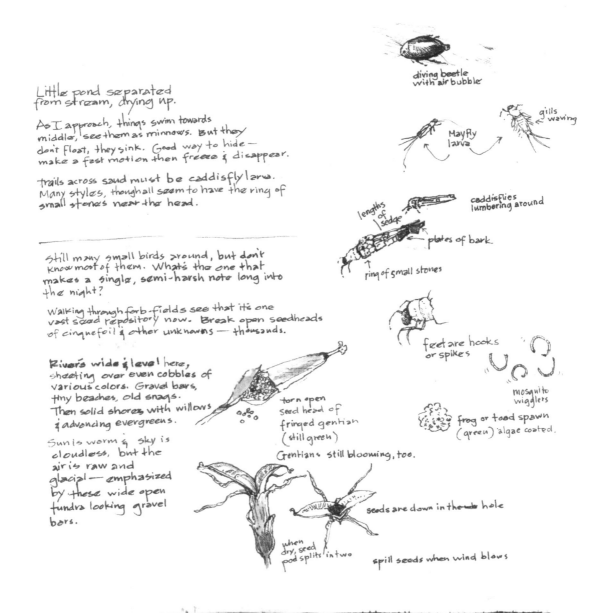

Little pond separated
from stream, drying up.

As I approach, things swim towards
middle, see them as minnows. But they
don't float, they sink. Good way to hide —
make a fast motion then freeze & disappear.

Trails across sand must be caddisfly larva.
Many styles, though all seem to have the ring of
small stones near the head.

diving beetle
with air bubble

MayFly
larva

gills
waving

lengths
of
sedge

caddisflies
lumbering around

plates of bark

ring of small stones

Still many small birds around, but don't
know most of them. What's the one that
makes a single, semi-harsh note long into
the night?

Walking through forb-fields see that it's one
vast seed repository now. Break open seedheads
of cinquefoil & other unknowns — thousands.

feet are hooks
or spikes

mosquito
wigglers

Rivers wide & level here,
sheeting over even cobbles of
various colors. Gravel bars,
tiny beaches, old snags.
Then solid shores with willows
& advancing evergreens.

torn open
seed head of
fringed gentian
(still green)

frog or toad spawn
(green) algae coated.

Gentians still blooming, too.

Sun is warm & sky is
cloudless, but the
air is raw and
glacial — emphasized
by these wide open
tundra looking gravel
bars.

when
dry, seed
pod splits in two

seeds are down in the hole

spill seeds when wind blows

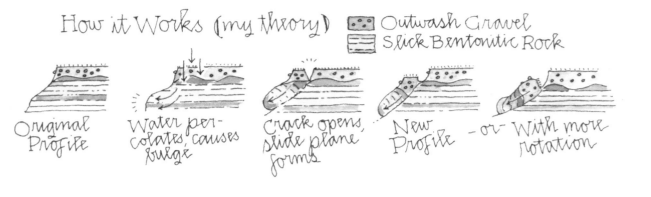

How it Works (my theory)
Outwash Gravel
Slick Bentonitic Rock

Original Profile

Water percolates, causes bulge

Crack opens, slide plane forms

New Profile

— or — With more rotation

Learning to differentiate: from *bird*, to *swallow*, to *barn swallow*, is a heady experience for the developing naturalist. Sometimes a taste of that knowledge can determine a future path. There is the person who can't collect enough names, who seeks out "firsts" and maintains ever-lengthening lists. There is another person, equally observant, to whom the interest in names comes after the knowledge of interactions. A person who has formed an affinity for a place will likely ask both "What's here?" and "What's going on here?"

Apprehending the world as events neatly circumvents the frustration of not knowing the names of things, a hurdle that can result in a feeling of alienation. Armed with the questions "What's going on?" and "What is it doing?" the watcher jumps right into the fray and gets caught up in the unfolding stories. This strikes me as a good way to introduce children to the world of nature, trusting that the riveting quality of event-perception will prompt more curiosity, and inspire some systematic learning. It develops a basic naturalist's skill, too: expecting the unexpected.

My own observations are also events—following the trajectory of my interest and curiosity. A little clump of phlox on the edge of the wash has come to my attention—an event. I can unfold that moment of interest indefinitely, until I have exhausted it, or until another event occurs to divert me. Such as this sudden hunch: the soil shelf that hosts the junipers might be there because at one time Sheep Leap Canyon was *dammed*—by more of the same cliff-face debris that still camouflages its entrance today.

Also, events that may have happened millions of years ago can become present again, as you read their traces in the current landscape. The wall of smooth, polished cobbles, not very well cemented together, is an exhumation of an ancient streambed. You can't trace in which direction it flowed from what is exposed here (at least I can't), but you know it was a pretty lively bit of water, judging by the size of the rocks it carried. Now those rocks, buried for who knows how many years (look it up when you get home) are back in the sunlight, and in fact fairly leaping out of the wall to go downstream again. That's what's happening. A sequence of almost childish little sketches would capture it.

When I lapse back into the culturally agreed-

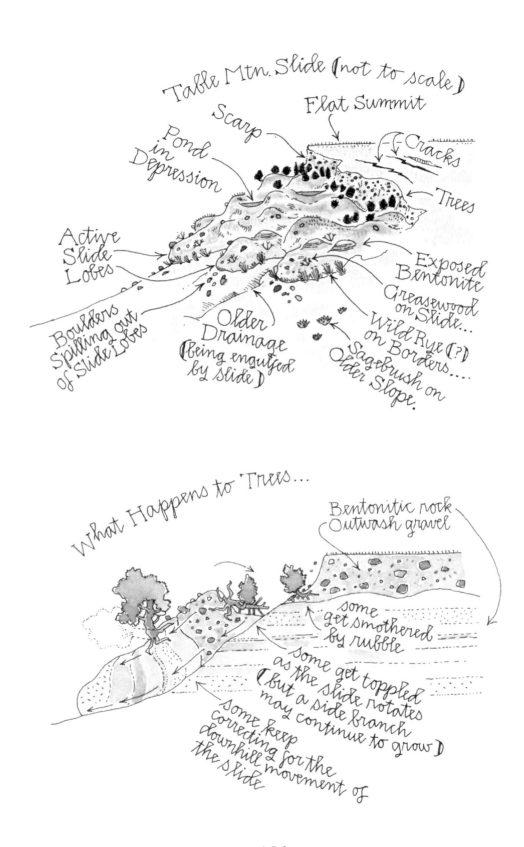

Table Mtn. Slide (not to scale)

Flat Summit

Scarp

Pond in Depression

Cracks

Trees

Active Slide Lobes

Exposed Bentonite

Greasewood on Slide...

Wild Rye (?) on Borders....

Boulders Spilling out of Slide Lobes

Older Drainage (being engulfed by slide)

Sagebrush on Older Slope.

What Happens to Trees...

Bentonitic rock

Outwash gravel

some get smothered by rubble

some get toppled as the slide rotates (but a side branch may continue to grow)

some keep correcting for the downhill movement of the slide

upon view of the world as inanimate (event perception is hard to maintain against that), I find that it seems false and unnecessarily dull. Choosing to live in a world of events, cultivating it as a way of seeing, means that I am likely to laugh at odd moments: a willow branch ducking in and out of high river water is a clown act. Cliff swallows assembling at a favorite mud puddle, ritually holding their wings aloft for a few seconds as they alight, is a glimpse into a secret society. Watching the progress of a distant rain-veil, enacted in silence, causes a sudden hush in the soul. A watcher in a world of events will be by turns startled, jubilant with discovery, puzzled and inflamed by curiosity, but never bored.

I'll devote several more hours to this kind of blissful puttering in the canyon, and then likely climb higher, to a place I've never explored before, unless a storm materializes. It would be nice to come away with some sketches or watercolors that will commemorate this singular day. And I'd love finally to find the crevice nest of a rock wren, which, according to Bent, includes a little walkway of stones, gathered and placed by the bird or birds (Which? Check Bent when you get home).

Inside this summer day are dramas of cloud and kestrel, roots and erosion, the tension in a desert primrose bud and its imminent release. Silty mud acts out its true nature as it dries and cracks along traditional lines. I don't want to miss any plot twist or virtuoso performance: everything is in motion.

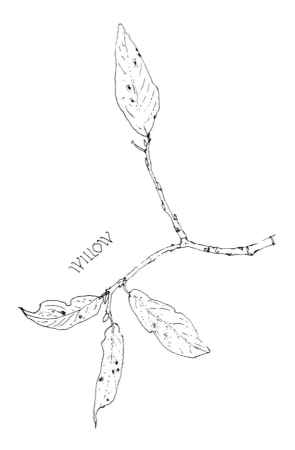

WILLOW

Diagram of small-sound tapestry in Soda Butte Valley
1. Distant hawk cry
2. Slow grasshoppers
3. Loud flying ratchet grasshoppers
4. Hum of bees & flies going by
5. Fast grasshoppers
6. Stream prinkling

Pebble
creeks
cave-like
coolness
generated
by swift
water being
aerated
over
boulders

dipper nest
on cliff
two nestlings near fledging
no—three
no—four!

155

One of the best ways I've found to participate in the world of events, and bring them into the journal, is through an Event Map. It's a simple mixing of words, images and symbols on a page, but it achieves things that drawing alone, or writing alone, seem to fall short of.

An Event Map is an actual map, in that it traces your route through a landscape, as you encounter it. It can be more or less complex in its attention to landforms, but usually it notes, or represents with illustrations or invented map devices, changes in altitude, terrain underfoot, stream crossings, basic vegetation patterns, and basic geology. You keep your eye on the larger landform story: What drainage? What microhabitats within this territory? How do creatures array themselves in your field of investigation? What rocks are exposed? What geologic events have shaped, are shaping, the place? This is especially important if it's a place you don't know well, or at all. I often study topographical maps of a new area, before or after I visit it, in order to add to my mental jigsaw puzzle of the wider territory.

An Event Map won't help you find your way back to a place, because it isn't drawn to scale, and its parts don't have to remain in proportion to each other. If I'm snared in a rich web of events alongside the stream, for example, that section of the map enlarges itself and becomes denser. However, if I make a special discovery, like a nest or a den, I'll try to include sight coordinates so that I can be sure to locate it again.

what's magpie eating in the yard?

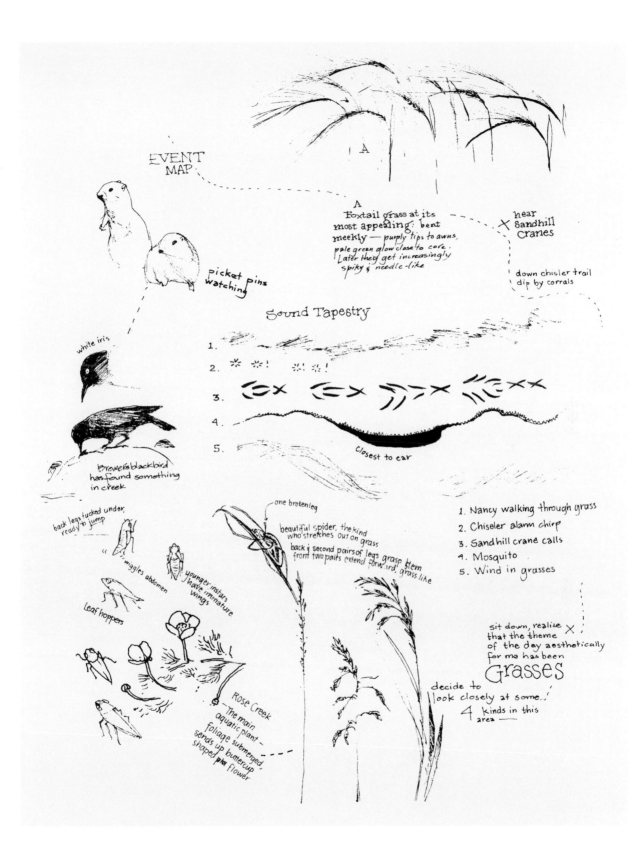

EVENT MAP

A
Foxtail grass at its most appealing: bent meekly — purply tips to awns, pale green glow close to core. Later they get increasingly spiky & needle-like

near Sandhill Cranes X

down chisler trail dip by corrals

picket pins watching

white iris

Brewer's blackbird has found something in creek

Sound Tapestry

1.

2.

3.

4.

5.

Closest to ear

back legs tucked under, ready to jump

wiggles abdomen

younger instars have immature wings

Leaf hoppers

one broken leg

beautiful spider, the kind who stretches out on grass

back & second pairs of legs grasp stem front two pairs extend forward, grass like

1. Nancy walking through grass
2. Chiseler alarm chirp
3. Sandhill crane calls
4. Mosquito
5. Wind in grasses

sit down, realize X that the theme of the day aesthetically for me has been

Grasses

decide to look closely at some.. 4 kinds in this area —

Rose Creek
— The main aquatic plant — foliage submerged. sends up buttercup shaped pale flower

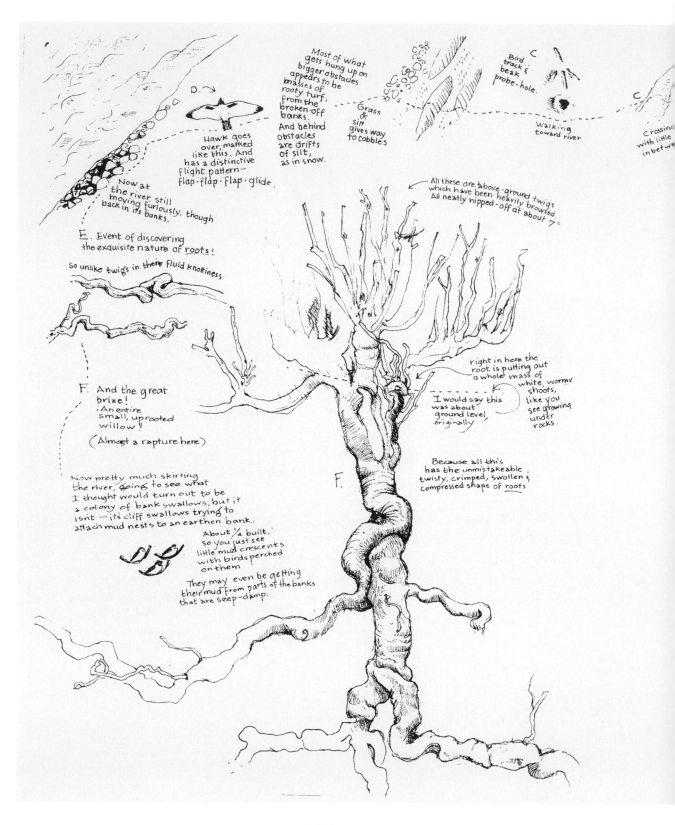

Most of what gets hung up on bigger obstacles appears to be masses of rooty turf, from the broken-off banks. And behind obstacles are drifts of silt, as in snow.

Grass & silt gives way to cobbles

Bird track & beak probe-hole.

Walking toward river

Crossing with little in betw...

C

C

D.

Hawk goes over, marked like this. And has a distinctive flight pattern — flap-flap-flap-glide.

Now at the river, still moving furiously, though back in its banks.

E. Event of discovering the exquisite nature of roots!

So unlike twigs in their fluid knottiness

F. And the great prize! · An entire small, uprooted willow! (Almost a rapture here)

Now pretty much skirting the river, going to see what I thought would turn out to be a colony of bank swallows, but it isn't — it's cliff swallows trying to attach mud nests to an earthen bank.

About ¼ built, so you just see little mud crescents with birds perched on them

They may even be getting their mud from parts of the banks that are seep-damp.

All these are above-ground twigs which have been heavily browsed. All neatly nipped-off at about 7".

right in here the root is putting out a whole mass of white, wormy shoots, like you see growing under rocks.

I would say this was about ground level, originally

F.

Because all this has the unmistakeable, twisty, crimped, swollen & compressed shape of roots

158

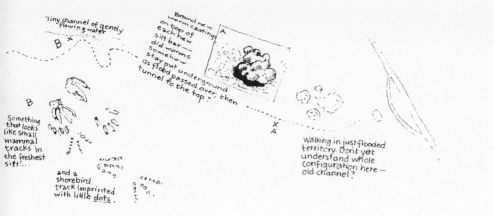

As maps go, it's more like the fifteenth-century *mappa mundi*, produced in the early stages of world exploration, heavily illustrated, with detailed insets of particular regions. And it certainly has ties with Australian aboriginal "songlines" that record time, sequence, and significance, as well as topography. Its purpose is to create a trail of encounters as you, the explorer, move through a particular place, at a particular moment, asking, "What's going on here?"

You are both active and passive in this exercise: active because you are alert, so certain things catch your eye, and may arrest you enough that your attention to them itself becomes an event. And passive, because things suddenly happen to you, in front of you, that are independent of your selective perception (unless heightened attention is some kind of a strange attractor for events).

An Event Map takes shape around a wandering line that mirrors your path, whether purposeful or erratic. Along it will appear symbols that mark the approximate site of an event, with at least a few words indicating what has happened, or is happening. Pulled out into the margins, or keyed by letters, numbers or some other method, might be a quick sketch, a careful drawing, or a play-by-play depiction in words, images, or invented notation.

Questions arise, and questions are events: make a note of your question along the trail, and what in your surroundings, if anything, prompted it. Some of your entries on the map will be brief, others will show signs of microscopic examination.

Right now, there's no need to know the names of anything you encounter, beyond being able to tell bird from insect. Because of your involvement, you'll probably yearn for names but save that for later, and concentrate now on "what's

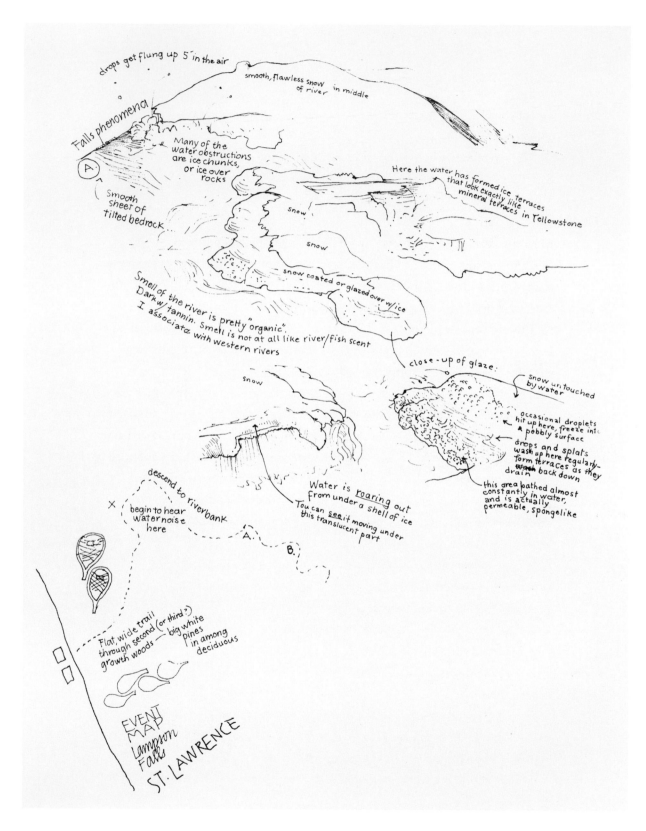

drops get flung up 5" in the air

smooth, flawless snow of river in middle

Falls phenomena

A.

Many of the water obstructions are ice chunks, or ice over rocks

Smooth sheer of tilted bedrock

Here the water has formed ice terraces that look exactly like mineral terraces in Yellowstone

snow

snow

snow coated or glazed over w/ice

Smell of the river is pretty "organic". Dark w/ tannin. Smell is not at all like river/fish scent I associate with western rivers

snow

close-up of glaze:

snow untouched by water

occasional droplets hit up here, freeze into a pebbly surface

drops and splats wash up here regularly— form terraces as they wash back down drain

Water is roaring out from under a shell of ice You can see it moving under this translucent part

this area bathed almost constantly in water, and is actually permeable, spongelike

descend to riverbank

X begin to hear water noise here

A.

B.

Flat, wide trail through second (or third?) growth woods — big white pines in among deciduous

EVENT MAP
Lampson Falls

ST. LAWRENCE

160

probably yearn for names but save that for later, and concentrate now on "what's going on."

The tendency when doing an Event Map, at least for me, is to come to a complete stop. If you find you can't go on, that there is too much occurring in your immediate vicinity, just let your route-line end in an explosion of images and observations. I call that a "Rapture." You'll probably be pretty well used up when the time comes to go back to your starting point, so don't feel compelled to map your route back. An Event Map with a Rapture is strange looking, harder to interpret as a map, but it remains true to experience.

More likely, you'll finish the day or the hour with an artifact that looks something like a game board, full of little detours, doublings-back, numbers and letters, enlarged areas, invented textures and patterns; impressions of movement, shape and gesture; and diagrams reminiscent of football plays. Part of the delight of the Event Map is its tendency to shift emphasis, style and scale according to the flow of events.

Looking back at a two-page event map from August, 1993 (reproduced as the endpapers of this book), in which most of the drawings are very simple, even cartoon-like, I can still unroll a whole string of vivid sense images from that day, many that aren't documented on the event map at all. All of these peripheral details, like the exact level of humidity, what I was wearing and which knapsack I

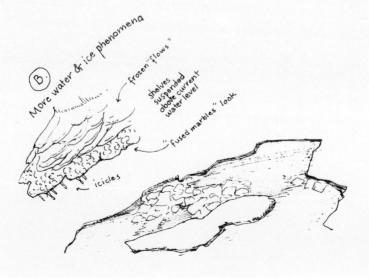

violet green
swallow nests

Meeting
place

X
note
exceptionally
springy turf

memory:
bee approaching
small blossom

discover
bumblebee
thorax is
much bidger
than abdomen

stopped
at pine tree
wondering
if I could
shake pollen
out of male
cones· no, they
are spent, dry &
very much ready to
fall off.

how
they look
on pine
branch

onto driveway

carried at the time, certain
fallen logs, the way voices sounded
in that little valley, and bits of conversation exchanged must be mysteri-
ously encoded on these pages, though they reside in
no particular drawing or phrase.

Event Maps have the power to reconstruct a
particular day for me more effectively than any
other form of recording I've found. Their power
may have to do with the fact that they preserve a
sequence, an unfolding of an adventure through time. Or
that they include odd details, not just the obvious categories of features we think we should
notice and link together. The aura of
the day and place somehow clings
to them with special
pungency.

Event map
in the
Ketchum
Woman's
garden

maple I dont
recognize with
clusters of keys

toothed all around

onto garden trail
now to draw a
penstemon ·
thousands of them in
this garden
(contour drawing)

a. peas
b. rhubarb
c. asparagus

kitchen garden

hundreds
of yellow
flowers

lower tier
trail

strawberries

event of hearing
what sounds like
bees getting stuck
in penstemon blossom
(high pitched, muffles buzzing
of wings inside flower)
but dont see it happen
— do notice that bees,
as they exit blossoms,
turn upside down &
do something to the
anthers· collect pollen?

grips flower with
legs

huge bee stuffing
himself into penstemon

162

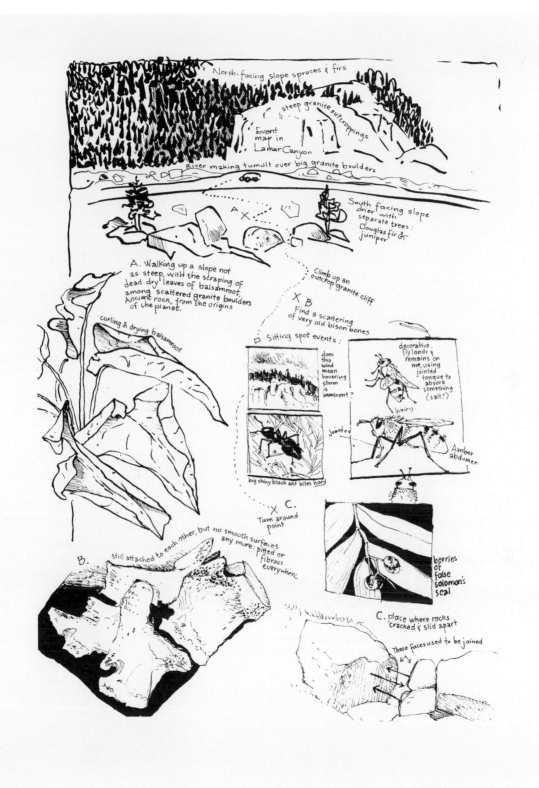

North-facing slope spruces & firs

steep granite outcroppings

Event map in Lamar Canyon

River making tumult over big granite boulders

South facing slope drier with separate trees: Douglas fir & juniper

A. Walking up a slope not as steep, with the scraping of dead dry leaves of balsamroot, among scattered granite boulders, Ancient rock, from the origins of the planet.

curling & drying balsamroot

Climb up an outcrop granite cliff

X B
Find a scattering of very old bison bones

☐ Sitting spot events:

does this wind mean hovering storm is imminent?

decorative. fly lands & remains on me, using jointed tongue to absorb something (salt?)

hairy

Jointed

Amber abdomen

big shiny black ant bites hard

X C.
Turn around point

still attached to each other, but no smooth surfaces any more: pitted or fibrous everywhere

B.

berries of false solomon's seal

C. place where rocks cracked & slid apart

These faces used to be joined

CHAPTER 9

TURNING THE YEARS' PAGES

Volume 1 *(Ohio, 1970)*

Saw the advancing cold front coming out of the west and heard great multitudes of red-wings and meadowlarks (?). The stage is set for spring and all the birds are calling to the earth to wake it up. Suddenly 4 or 5 woodcocks all begin peenting at once from various points in surrounding fields. What a funny noise it is! I can just see the fat little bird sitting out there with a bad cold, just kind of peenting around to himself. Then he takes off and starts wheeling around in circles making a wittering noise. You can never see him in the air. Then he'll stop wittering and begin descending making warbly noises. Nope, you can't see him then either, but you can follow the noise down to where it stops. Of course he then starts peenting again, in back of you or something.

Volume 2 *(Ohio, 1971)*

August 24th . . . My campers this week are dis-appointing. They're all fourteen, typically fourteen and are pretty oblivious to everything but themselves. Last night there were owls, some far away and one quite close and loud that I could not and cannot identify. I've got to find out what the bird is that sounds like a raccoon, and make sure I know all these bizarre woodpecker calls. I love woodpeckers, they are so ridiculous with their silly calls and hammering holes in trees. Woodpecker reply: Do you have a tongue so long you've got to curl it around your skull once? Don't knock it if you haven't tried it.

Volume 3 *(Ohio, 1972)*

December 6th . . . A really fine weekend again including an outing to the zoo. There were animals there whose skin looked to be made of couches and car upholstery, namely hippos and rhinopre-posterouses. There were two ugly saggy elephants that I didn't like until one tried to give a trunkful of hay to his fiancée. Oh, my, the apes made me uncomfortable with their human eyes and stripped-to-the-most-elemental human actions.

And then the cats, the exotic medium sized cats: child leopards, soft and beautiful and a nervous tightly caged leopard. It tore my heart to watch him frantically search for an exit and try to enact a hunting sequence in a 6' x 6' cage. But my favorites were the cougars. There was a thoroughly limp furry child cougar being washed by his mom. He would just roll around whichever way her tongue pushed him, big soft paws floundering around. The big apes were funny but upsetting in their decidedly threatening human qualities.

Volume 5 *(Florida, 1972)*

Corkscrew Swamp Sanctuary—There are alligators here, and great ponderous wood storks, the last in the country. Hawks and owls and warbler confetti. Here I am alone with the last wood storks in the country. They are about 4 feet tall with a wingspan of 6 feet. The young in the nest sound like millions of kids blowing birthday party horns. You can hear them snapping their bills together. The parents are breaking twigs to use in their nests. The sound of their wings is VERY VERY loud.

The little blue heron walking on pond lettuce is so graceful—long toes that work on the snowshoe principle. He is following a turtle who is crawling through the lettuce leaving a lane of water behind him. This is a good place for the heron to find minnows. Now there are people here, taking movies and interrupting. They all seem to know a lot about birds.

Volume 10 *(Ithaca, New York, 1974)*

Each day is a story telling itself (just a little

tale). Today was leaf-scrape day sounding like card houses falling down. A day just like all the others except that sometimes I'm seeing it as though I were just born.

Stream at our feet, wind milling above our heads. There go the last oakleaves! . . . with a shriek above the boughs. Stream snaking, groping below. Above, kinglet band scattering through tossing needles, little bell-voices blowing away. The rocks hold still as rocks, becoming their own stillness. The colors, the form of the hemlocks, palms down gesture, swaying like kilts. Bronze and copper leaves, some gleaming up from the bottom of the water.

Volume II *(Ithaca, 1975)*

The clarity of air and brilliance of colors! The Mae West abundance of flowers and unfurling

June 15
Arrive down
in warm
springs
canyon under sleet
squalls - but we
throw together
a handsome

camps with a fire,
coffee, burgers all in
a lush riverbend hunk
of land (callirhoe)
A restorative nap and
I'm leaving a ragged
past. Wilderness needs
to have you in sleep a
couple of times before
you "cross the border
into a land where
you do not live."

Much history to be
traveled over in the next
few days and I aim
to be aimless: wander,
putter, gaze, doze, sketch.
Get down scraps of
this recent past. Get
some glimpses of this
healing dose of mountain
days.

167

WINTER TIPI.

axe
draw knife
tape measure
hammer

what for liner?
water system
heat
working
sleeping
cooking/food
friends
flooring
refrigeration
storage
light
door

liner **
write nomadics tipi   Mother Earth News
find out about other tipi people.
how they live!
insulation between cover & liner - fiberglas??
Is it flammable?
                blankets liner?

Water - enough for cooking, washing, drinking
  Barrels?
  crocks?

Trading newspapers
Plastic containers with spigots

Heat ~ little parlor stove like brian and
barbaras & ask them
W.E.C. Trading papers
junk places, hdware stores

On brick & base

How to get stovepipe out &
where? out back
How to insulate?

Ask Yosemite
how they fix all their
canvas bldgs.

Refrigeration- Hole

sawdust

strawmats
barrel
rugs
hides
foam mattress
crock-barrel-jug
big aluminum container
chairs
old cabinet-
little old wood table sawed off
stove stove pipe
Kerosene lamp

• sand covered with
  straw mats
  rugs, hides

least contrived

How did Hunter
Valley folk get
poles to stay
put on platform?

16
Flooring - bricks?
sand? Boards?

```
  16
  12
  32
  16
  192
   24
 8 )192
   16
   32
```

24 2"x 8" with 2"x 4"
studs on the back later
Draw the diameter
then saw each board

Reassemble inside.
put sawdust layer
under? Too fire dangerous.
Sand? Stones?

working-
pigeonholed bookshelved box with
hinged thing to let down for a desk

sleeping ~
4 inch foam to roll up, tie & store
  or cover & use as
      cushion

Heavy top over all

4'

screen

aluminum
container
thermometer
screen
block of ice

let down into hole
Read of different methods

leaves, the trees like stained glass at Six Mile Creek this morning. All the plants had jewelled rims. They were so well watered in yesterday's storms that they had to expel the extra water in their bodies in the form of droplets from the edge of the leaves. Tried to climb a cliff but it was too sheer. Got lost and found a waterfall with a veery singing his version of it. Alone, and content.

Volume 12 *(Ithaca, 1975. Set up a tipi on my friends' land)*

Noonday. Sun is drenching my tipi clearing. Drying mats and bedding. I'm watching all those flourishing weeds thinking of the molecule chain circulation going on and the chloroplasts "hanging like sausages" from the roof of the inside of the leaf. Those velvety black damselflies are darning around. They are streamside summer. Saw my local garter snake stalking in the weed jungle. Sticks his head under some oak leaves and emerges with one of those spiny spiders.

Everything in the tipi is stained and dirty now, though, sort of mottled, getting to blend with the bare earth floor. The floor of my home is earth. I'm right on it. Down below are thousands of miles of foundation, down to a hot core.

Austere life here. My hands are dirty and cut and calloused from work. My tennis shoes are to an extreme stage of broken-inness, they are molded to my feet. My clothes are filled with smoke and sweat and dirt. I've learned what food works well here, and how to build a fine fire. (I know it's better to not be so careful and architectural about a fire.) Learned how to wield an axe and dig a good hole. No more fear in the dark woods. Learned how to walk in the dark, loose. (Still can never find the path from stream edge to the tipi in the dark though.) Being alone all the time lets me appreciate people when I'm with them. Today while I was gone a little wasp built a nest in the E hole of my recorder.

Volume 16 *(Earlham College, Indiana, 1976)*

Found a ridge and an apt beech tree; climbed. Nothing makes you remember better how your kid-body felt than climbing a tree. Saw a fine Indiana vale with characteristic sycamores—tans and reds of winter twigs plus osage orange's distinctive greenish-brown coloring and multiple-arched branches. Rocked in the top limbs of the beech. Not a flexible tree, that's why their tops get blown off, perhaps. Admired the beech's held leaves from last winter, and undid a bud. Found the tiny nubs of leaves with their fur much longer than and surrounding them. The fur that spreads out as the leaf expands. Admired beech gray and the creaking of branches in the wind, woods' winter song.

Volume 17 *(Earlham College, 1976)*

Haiku to go with paintings. Big schematic canvases using designs of emerging leaves. Series of little botanical drawings. Same problems as before

but some surprisingly sturdy and varied works. Horse chestnut on rice paper. Snow landscape with some unity. Sumi view from the bee hill. Mushroom hunters. Osprey. What's ahead: African tapestry, wood planer, emerging shoots. I love how these paintings are not chosen, their subjects are images I have been carrying with me, they are part of my life, like the leaves and the mushroom hunters, from spring and Ithaca.

We've just finished a glorious frisbee game inside our tree-walled field. How grand it is to hold the frisbee so comfortably and will your strength to uncoil in a snap, making it sail flat for a long distance. And then catching the frisbee: as it floats you are gauging it, judging its speed and speed you must reach to converge with it. Judging its height and how fast it's descending, deciding to leap for it or to run along and carefully remove it from the air, Michael's specialty.

Walking around campus under the newly dense trees after rain on a foggy flowery May night. Bridges, small lamplit scenes, compositions, sounds of wet footsteps.

But all this writing is being done at the coffee shop waiting for a burger!

Volume 19 *(Ohio, 1976)*

Sweet trusting cat who lived beneath the back porch during the –17 weather, that Mom and Dad wouldn't take in—had her spayed so there would be no more kittens. Kind vet said an Amish farmer would take her for a barn cat so I drove out there. Through the window I could see a table surrounded by folk, bonneted women.

As I opened the door to the milkhouse with the frightened cat in my arms, three children materialized around me. The girls wore plain long dresses with a sort of blazer coat, equally plain. They led me to the barn with no concern for the mud. They showed me the milk vat, half full of milk. Startling to see a whole lake of milk like that, with cat tracks on the lid of the vessel. Such an austere cold and windy gray day, spitting pellets of snow. Arriving at this farm in the deepest of Ohio agricultural land, far from the mainstream of the world, and meeting these youngsters, plain as the winter landscape, but with faces like young peaches, smooth as fresh-shelled beans, like sprouts in winter. I couldn't ask for anything better for the cat. It is a snug barn, the children are gentle and all the other cats are named.

Volume 20 (*Sharon Audubon Center, Sharon, Connecticut, 1977)*

Pine Plains marsh at 3:45 a.m. with huge cumuli of mist ascending against the background mountain, and 5000 redwings combining their liquid "conquer"s and their squalled "rees". We were waiting by the flowed lands on a dirt road, for rails, gallinules, bitterns, those secretive witch-voiced marsh birds. You must be all alertness to sift a bittern's croak out of the din of redwings. Never forget the vast fields with the sun rising through vapors, and how it colored the broad-faced mountain's spring woods.

Swallows in a sandbank, holes making a fine design, sand marked with brushes of swallows' wings and scrabbling of the feet. Connecticut valleys with free running streams and marshes. Humans building their dens in imaginative yet practical spots on the hillside, pleasing. But then the wealth that perched them there probably comes from the toil of a thousand people who live in a hideous development where a N.J. coastal marsh used to be.

Catbird mumbles to himself, a private, almost nonsensical conversation in the apple tree. On the other hand oriole declaims to the whole area. His comments sound like directions, or epithets from the grandstand. Maybe that's why his voice always makes me feel like something fun is going on in the yard. "Here, here! Throw it over here!" "Hello, welcome to the yard here!"

Barn swallows, the pair that nests in the garage,

through binoculars

barn swallow opens his mouth _wide_ when he does _the_ buzzy part of his song....

keep darting over talking in the wheezy way that some attractive women have—Lauren Bacall types. If they had human features they would have eyes that crinkle when they smile. Goldfinches talking say "chew-ee??" like a three-year-old. Everything in the landscape is sweet, gentle, charming, reassuring, comfortable.

With the decision to go to Wyoming, a new channel opens so that my affections begin to flow westward and ties become unbound here. Going again, this time more seriously. My base may be shifting to Wyoming and the pull east would wane and so will all that means so much to me here now. From Connecticut to Ohio feels like familiar territory, with Ithaca in between, no great journey. But even Ohio to Wyoming is vastly far—across the strange gulf of the great plains, alien to me. What will happen?

Volume 23 *(Wyoming, 1978)*

Five days into my 6-day solitary mountain trip. The Girl who Walked Over Continental Glacier is

searching on Whiskey Mountain for a tent-spot out of the 40 mph gusts. Wandering over complex mountain geology till I find a rocky site at the foot of a geode-filled dolomite outcropping. Practice: slow down your vision till you can actually see the clouds traveling on their planes of air. So far only breezes here, but cold like on the peak, with that wind off Ram Flat. My view is drawn on the next pages: within sight of the harrowing ice and boulder land I've just come through.

It will take a long time, maybe years, to determine what frightened me so much about the divide. A terrified loneliness. Didn't even eat—

went to sleep with a hunk of dark chocolate in my hand, thinking I'd better stoke some fuel to burn in the night, but I didn't eat it. Woke up with it melted all over me. I expected to hike right back down Arrow Mountain the next morning. Instead, somehow, went forward.

Geology! Someone explain what these layers are, why geodes, why fossils—why granite on west side and sedimentary on this side?

Even in the huge gusts, spent about 45 minutes on the summit with my map, picking out the Dunoir, Horse Creek and Wiggins Fork country —the East Fork and Bear Creek drainages—Black

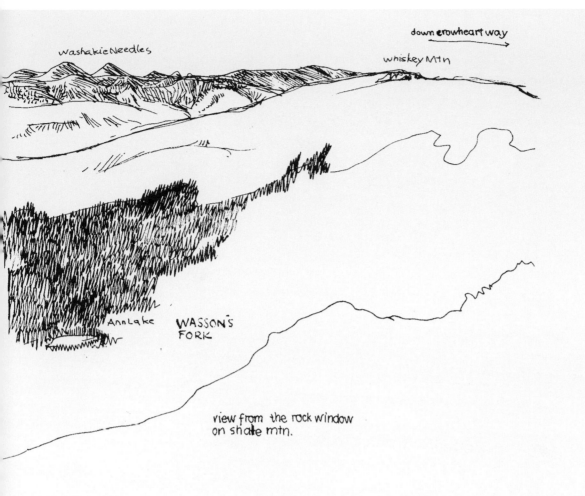

washakie Needles

down crowheart way

whiskey Mtn

Ann Lake   WASSON'S
FORK

view from the rock window
on shale mtn.

Mountain complex and tiny Crowheart Butte, casting a long shadow.

Volume 24 (*Ohio, 1978*)

Home to Ohio for Christmas. Brother Lew quotes Heidegger: "Nossingness lies at ze heart of being, like a verm." I read aloud, from Arthur Cleveland Bent, on wood ducks: "in the over-flowed, heavily wooded bottoms of our great interior rivers, where rising waters have half submerged and killed the forest trees, this pretty little timberland duck finds a congenial home among the half sunken snags, stumps and dead trees." No verm here!

Poor Ohio. That familiar feeling of desperation when I see thousands of new houses covering some of the richest farmland in the country, new developments sprawling in all directions. Ohio's colors look shabby and dull to me. I realized as we wound around the cloverleaf on the outer belt that they look that way because the natural integrity of forests, fields and rivers has been broken up so much that there is no way left to imagine how a woods edge would have looked going off to the river without the garish colors of tract houses and cars.

I mentioned to Lew how it has changed me to finally comprehend watersheds. He agreed, saying it was the West that had taught him, too. Then Lew and I exercised our watershed consciousness by applying it to Kettering, Ohio, where we grew up. We noticed that Kettering must have been on a major trail between the Miami River and its tributary the Little Miami, because they come so near each other at that point. And I was never really aware of either of them, growing up.

Volume 25 (*Wyoming, 1979*)

Claritas, wedgewood, cerulean to indigo, dustless, polished, precious stone, transparent enamel, cobalt stained glass—blue grape hyacinth wine sky.

I'm wanting to be beautiful to go with it. Wanting to dance, win hearts. Win *a* heart. Looking for that deeply shared intimacy.

The wedding in Hudson—managed to borrow the elegant and spirited Scirocco for this event. Got all dandied up again, in the new palm tree and Bahama-blue dress. Hudson full of vehicles, whole town being fed homemade "Sarma" in the back room of the Union Bar, and a roast pig. Serbian food and songs.

I went back and forth inside and out drinking beer, talking delightedly with anyone I ran into, watching, rarely feeling awkward. Sunny, windy dusk. Left alone, half drunk, after a few grand polkas with the old men in the hideously lit back room.

I feel the elation of traveling along, light as a dragonfly, towards the mountains I never tire of. Started singing a song of love to them, with wild enthusiasm and abandon. Driving slowly, the Lyons Valley Road utterly empty and quiet.

Passing a pond with ducks, redwings, tall reeds, I stop short, jump out laughing, ebullient, stumbling, and begin fiercely reaping last year's reeds, about 7 feet tall. That must be when I ripped my dress. Next time I looked, my hand was dripping blood and it was falling on the wonderful blue dress. Cuts from pulling reeds fiercely.

Volume 27 (*Wyoming, 1980*)

Home through icy streets tonight in the last of dusk. Snow starting to fall. In front of the old farmhouse, the one with pigeons, saw, through the branches of the fruit tree, lit rooms. Something about the scene . . . . a woman stirring something. The light is yellow, it's not modern. A patch of old flowery wallpaper. What I felt had to do with Christmas as well as that "old time" sense that I think comes to me from some distant past. Christmas . . . . night . . . . lights . . . . remember the absolute wonder of driving around Upper Arlington with my parents, small, looking at the lights, transposed to another world. The crowning event being the castle (it seemed to me then) outlined in *blue* lights. Blue lights lining the driveway —it seemed to go up a mountainside.

Volume 28 (*Portland, Maine, Portland School of Art, 1980*)

Boursin and good coffee at Cafe Domus.

A morning after class of wandering through the city, finally achieving a relaxed and unhurried stroll. Into stores full of treasures, making small purchases, ringing up a tally in my head of five times more than I actually walk out with. Beginning to grasp what the particular beauty of this place is. I found it this a.m. in the bright

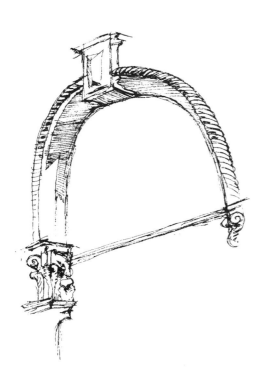

September water and the cormorant waking up, flapping, splashing. The city rising up above the ferry dock, facing east, catching light on windows. Fresh heavy autumn dew from a cool night—we have to wipe the ferry benches.

Exchange St.—rows of healthy maples making the narrow street feel like a little "bois". Brick details dense above the front doors, in perspective along the street, a sense of Dickensian ornateness. Wake up everyone! Don't you see your exquisite right-size city here in its bright new season?

Now with my several more hours, I'll try to find a spot to sit and draw, try to catch a few details. Here, instead of the pattern of a swallow's wing, draw the brick elaboration over a casement window.

Poor David overwhelmed by his chowder-making. Misery attending that chowder anyway, because the lobsters had been dying all day in their small freshwater prison-bucket. I don't want to do that to animals anymore.

Volume 29 *(Peaks Island, Maine, 1980)*

The thing recollected: bird day alone. Where the road goes across woods, stop and call in some small birds in a pine stand. They gather near— chickadees, golden-crowned kinglets, and a red-breasted nuthatch who really inspected me, first one eye, then the other. At that moment a strong reaffirmation of at-homeness, alone, on earth.

Gathering mussel shells alone, but not alone. Good company: the one who walks on the rocks, and the One who *enjoys* the one who walks on the rocks.

A loon, a loon! Binoculars out to see. A varnished wooden sailboat in a gold fog, far off. That image has persisted and grown more powerful.

Volume 33 *(Maine, 1982)*

As you get older you exchange the fervor of your initial discoveries for a richness of knowledge, wider experience. Wider experience implies ambivalence. Fewer instant passionate judgments or decisions. Am still mourning the passing of the initial fervor.

Volume 34 (*Maine, 1982*)

Bird songs come and go in waves. They'll all be quiet for a while except maybe the catbird who doesn't follow rules, or the vireo who drones on anyway. Then everyone will be singing—thrushes, warblers, flycatchers, grosbeak. Peaks Island wood thrushes have particularly clarion notes. Clear abrupt phrases, like a poet with line-by-line inspiration. Sinking into a morning of bird-listening like a frazzled tired person into a leisurely bath.

Chickadee nearby making the noise that sometimes precedes a visit to my head, to pull out hairs for its nest.

Volume 35 (*Maine, 1983*)

Focus on controlling temper, emotion. Oh, but when in the throes, the urges erupt before the motions to suppress them can intercede.

Talk about it as though I am weak, have faint sense of self. Not so. Extremely strong ego—basically generous but when wounded or fallen behind, like now, it is full of undifferentiated rage and venom. Demanding, absorbed with life drama.

Part of passion of youth is that better part of the energy (admired by those who don't have it

Sept 7

The enormous raven cloud rears up above Yellowstone on the day of the high winds.

We think it is the Huck Fire. Pushed by due west gales, it will reach the southern part of the blowdown in the Teton Wilderness.

No word on Cooke(d) city or Old Faithful Lodge. Waiting up to hear the late news.

This is the summer of the firestorm; fires of a magnitude never seen before (but building up in the form of downed fuel for decades) in this region.

The park is radically changed. How will it recover physically?

Watching the clouds of fireweed seeds parachuting by at the Bonneville pass trailhead—will wager that Yellowstone's burned-over district will be a sea of pink next year.

Correlation between fireweed's enthusiastic blooming in very dry years with it's success next year on the lands burned in that same dry year.

anymore) is just the thrill of being unquestioned center stage, lead role in the great hit of their own lives. Later, they see that the audience has left, is asleep, or worse that there isn't an attentive audience, just countless dramas played to empty houses . . . .

The "abandoned" feeling of fall. In the summer, places belong to humans, are laden with human attention. Now any old rocky corner has an air of wilderness because it's left alone. These fall processes—migrators threading the brush, ferns browning—all seem especially lonely and wild. The light contributes: dim, antique, yellow—and the small bell-like sounds the migrators make in passing.

There is that maple syrup/smoke, "wasp nest" smell in the air right now. Started examining what is so remarkable about fall colors. Not just trees, but what the hot-hued leaves do to the color of the sky. When trees are yellow and orange, the sky adds an overtone of violet. Could that be it?

From Margot's letter, a quote from George Eliot:

". . . there is no short cut, no patent tram-road, to wisdom: after all the centuries of invention, the soul's path lies through the thorny wilderness which must still be trodden in solitude, with bleeding feet, with sobs for help, as it was trodden by those of old times."

Volume 37 (Maine, 1983)

Down with straw mat to the water. Red granite through blue surface = garnet and agate. A. Clampitt's poem, the "bloodied bath of Agamemnon" refers to same.

Unsteady on the rocks. Go down to rising water.

Feet in, shock, then used to it. Lean over tide pool. Lovely pink and white crabs, other brown and green ones, none more than quarter-sized. Shrimp things en masse. Closer, watch bladder-weeds swaying heavily, fleshy belly dancers. Lobsterman thrums by, traps going off the back. Blue buoy.

Watching the weight and heft, scales tipping, shifting, pouring, brimming-filling of the water. All its movements definite, lusty, vital, unhesitant. My life and works: little dry feeble scratchings. Nothing with full heft to it.

Yesterday, after a gentle dawn thunderstorm, there were fog banks and tendrils of fog which burned off under classically perfect late summer day. Thought upon waking this morning and hearing the catbird—his song is typed all on punctuation keys.

Volume 38 (Wyoming, 1984)

About river dipping. Some things to know about getting out in the middle of a mountain river hurling over boulders. Use hands, lean into current obliquely and brace with feet against solid rocks. Move slowly, one limb at a time. Don't get swept away unless you've looked it over, know you have a clear chute and can get out of the current via piece of flat water.

Ah, out there. The sculptural presence of water! That 2-foot thick sluice of water hauling over the boulder appears solid, transparent. Stick your hand in trout-wise and feel what velocity does to magnify weight. Turn hand against the current and control thick fountains, sheet arcs, French curves and notice the space created behind, under your fountain; an air space surrounded by a solid. Water is not drippy here, but heavy crystal volumes, only occasionally broken and aerated.

In the white froth. Pearly bubble fizzing, but also pummelings of variable currents, condensing and rearranging muscles and flesh. Listen for the bass drumming in the water.

Volume 39 (*Maine, 1985*)

Something strangely visionary about this motionless chalky white day. Maybe it's pre-collapse caffeine vision.

Snow stands trampled, inert. There is a sort of whitish fog, mostly apparent as it shrouds distances in a milky blueness, starchy. Gull goes over, muted and indistinct against gull-colored sky. No brilliance or transparency in the landscape. Not that there are no colors, but that they sit heavy and opaque. Green of the St. Christopher's Second Hand Shop, like a rest home turned inside out. Horrendous blue of the plumber's house.

Sounds all very distinct. Water of bay perfectly flat, listless. This kind of day should be depressing, but it's so remarkable in its ugliness that it doesn't affect one that way. Kind of day Louise Bogan talked about in Massachusetts mill towns.

Volume 40 (*Wyoming, 1985*)

Finley and me riding to the lofty meadows up on South Pass on two borrowed horses, our job is to move cows to another pasture. Swales filled with violets and wild iris. Wet beneath too, sweet sound of hooves in the muck. One gallop, but mostly wandering under the galleon clouds, sending shadows over us. Cool sweeps of wind and floating raptors.

One particular moment, when we'd herded the 30 or so cows into a bunch—light gleaming on their shining hides, dust blowing up a little—

Finley slouching, me on the gray—we don't talk for a long time.

Close to heaven.

Volume 42 (*Wyoming, 1986*)

Ice on the lake is moving in this sudden thaw—60 degrees. Smart cracks, and longer groans. Somehow you can hear the planar surface in the cracks. An underlying tone, going on almost constantly, a drone, that sounds a bit like a distant prop plane.

Many ice varieties along the edge of the lake. A top layer of intersecting ice needles, above a layer of water, above a smooth sheet of ice. In the smooth ice, extremely precise trails of little bubbles. They look silver, in a black field.

A delicate plate of ice, about $\frac{1}{32}$ of an inch thick, with ice needles growing *down* from its underside, in horizontal clumps like bundles of pine needles.

The ice is making huge adjustments. When it cracks at this end, the water-margin at the edge of the ice-sheet trembles. Groans come from the edge, near, then traveling away.

Big ice cracks scare the Clark's nutcrackers and make them cry out.

Volume 44 (*Wyoming, 1987*)

Scout turning into an impressive colt, after getting over his spoiled, Arabian-Ranch upbringing. Riding with Michael, deeper into the mountains than I would go alone. To Shoshone Pass, and then finding a route up for my first glimpse of the Absaroka Plateau. Leading horses through talus piles with brilliant alpine flowers impressing themselves on my oxygen-starved consciousness: forget-me-not, sky pilot, a big woolly sunflower-looking

FEB 3

Thirty-seven below last night. No vehicles will start. Magpies have a rim of ice around their eyes.

Clark's nutcracker must have gotten hungry for a hot drink. Caught a chickadee and took it fluttering down to the river snow and ice, giving it gentle stabs in the breast.

Michael fed our ponies 2 extra bales of hay at 9:30 last night, and spread out a bale beneath the birdfeeder. But no deer or moose tracks.

Still no wind, thank god, & with sun it's warmed up to −25°. I can't stop thinking about the suffering of creatures exposed to this. What about calving, at its height right now? Be thrown into −30°, wet? You couldn't survive. You'd freeze to the ground. What are they doing?

This strange arctic wave is moving slowly, and penetrating in an unusual way — Panhandle Texas is zero this morning, but it hasn't gotten into the midwest yet. And Jackson of all places, was only zero yesterday, while we were −20°. It's a bowl and had its lid on. But now it's dropping there too.

Even though I'm warm, I can't relax, though work will distract me. (Finishing Geoff's map today) What if this becomes a pattern for the winter?

At 10:50, it's warmed up to an amazing −18°, on the shady side. Surely in direct sun animals can get warm even if the air is cold...

181

Rockwren - dweedle-eedle-eedle-eedle......
chukky-chukky-chukky-chukky...
chu-DEE chu-DEE chu-DEE......

VIOLET-GREEN

182

JULY 7

Have ascended to
a white-layer camel back
saddle — scary climb wedging
feet in crumbly crack.

whine of D. Wilson's mill &
wasp-in-a-bottle snarl of dirtbikes.
Squalling ravens. Violet green
swallows in & through & over the
structures.

Wildly varied gravel getting
washed out of certain
badlands layers. speckled
pink granite, black & white
speckles too. white quartz.
Black & red banded. Deep
red with fine glitter. smooth
pale green.

On the steep washed flanks:
a layer of silt cemented in a bumpy
drip-flow pattern.   If you break
that off, under-   neath is
a flowing, sifted   pocket of
red sand & under that,
a flow of blue gray
sand, loose & streaming down.
They're getting washed away but there are many
deposition events in the process too.

sun hot but air
cold; my body
goes to uncom-
fortable ex-
tremes.

Finally learned
that one flat
spot on a
red clay
butte was
warm &
comfortable
if I
lay down —
and dropped
off into
a blissful
floating

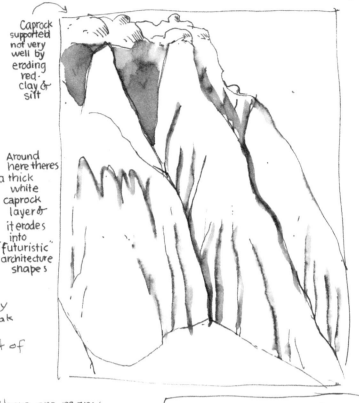

Caprock
supported
not very
well by
eroding
red-
clay &
silt

Around
here theres
a thick
white
caprock
layer &
it erodes
into
"futuristic"
architecture
shapes

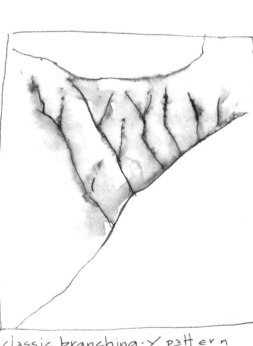

classic branching-y pattern

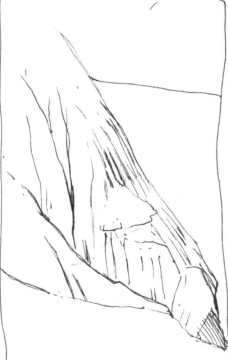

thing (Townsendia). Wind, snow and brilliance on the summit. Got a sense of the plateau distances; on top, you can't see into the deep canyons striking in on all sides, so it looks like an unbroken plain. Found another route down—across a steep, extensive snowfield, leading Scout! He's collected, though he realizes the peril.

We scan a distant mountainside with binoculars. M. discerns a cow elk with a very small dun-colored blur near her. She grazes up the slope, little dun spot stays put. Then we spy large bird, must get its scale—yes, it is a golden eagle, making a pass at the hillside. Suddenly cow elk comes tearing across, on the scene: elk calf almost taken.

Volume 45 (Wyoming, 1989)

Have this whole day to myself, and approach it with relieved deliberation, the kind of "mindfulness" that smoothes jagged edges and restores luminosity to everything. Wandered outside with coffee because I heard a bluebird. Love those quiet, low-pitched notes—don't think they're capable of a harsh sound. Decided to pick some spinach leaves, put them in the salad spinner. So I'm crouched in the garden, sun warm, air cool, listening to the bluebird notes, admiring the soil, still moist from its last watering, and snipping shiny spinach leaves.

Turned faucet on to run cold water into bucket with greens, wished a moment that I had some robin's-egg-blue speckled enamel washtub to soak those greens in. Sensation of cold water pouring into and spilling over bucket rim and my hands sloshing around in there. Smell of hot boards suddenly wet. Spinach live and crisp! Awake!

Saw that the airy breezeway, now cluttered with winter's chopping block and wheelbarrow, would be the cool and shady place to read, so cleaned and swept it, and placed a rocking chair and a rug out there, and sat right down in the rocker to read Richard Ford's story "Rock Springs". Chair and horse blanket look so beautiful—red, black and white blanket with shining black cat asleep on it.

Volume 48 (Wyoming, 1991)

Last night finding the new trail. And watching the grouse balancing clownishly on the top of the osier twigs, plucking white berries. That seemed nothing less than a miraculous gift—realizing that no matter how bitter the worldly circumstances, I can still see and participate in the small things out here. And now, a woodpecker tapping behind me and an occasional dry leaf coming down. Other goods: call to Lucy, and from Claudia. Reappearance on the scene of SarahSarah, who once again opens my heart right up. You need some friends of different ages. Women 60+, at whose kitchen tables you sit. "Pluck." Isn't that the word E. B. White quoted from E. M. Forster? An unspoken, unacknowledged fraternity of people with "Pluck."

Volume 50 (Wyoming, 1993)

To Byrd Draw. Lower end hammered by cows. Cow dung—inert mountains of it—looks so inefficient, artificial even. Won't disperse, doesn't scatter, just sits there ossifying, intact for years. And all vegetation between sagebrush gone.

Up the first side canyon, where despair overtook me. Climbed around, though, looking for flat slab of trysting sandstone—no level surface in the entire canyon. Up a slot, and in real danger trying

Deep forest above McDonald Creek —
boulders almost entirely moss-clad —
two and three inches deep in a variety
of mosses. They can be pulled off like a
skin, but you don't want to do that —
it's intriguing enough to reach in two fingers
through a hole and slide them between moss and
rock, always damp. They emerge smelling of
dirt from a dream garden — humus emanation.
I know that among the trees here are western red cedar,
whose bark I can tell at a distance, and western hemlock.
All the young trees seem to be hemlock & cedar, but
of the big ones — and they're not so much big around
as they are tall — it's only cedar that I know
for sure. Superb bark textures — plates,
strips and blocks. Mosses, lichens,
hemlock needles, pine needles and
cedar panicles cover all the ground —
including rocks and the older downed
timber. About three inches down
you find a blackened
compost, most of the
plant matter by now
unrecognizeable,
shot through
with
mycelia.

A U G U S T 21
               20

O V E R C A S T

C O O L

3:00 pm

to climb out. Realized that vaguely, but kept singing Lucinda Williams songs, made some quick weight-shift moves above abysses, the kind that have your whole balance pivoting past two fingers on a tiny, unsteady rock. Tried to draw, but monstrous shadow of panic and worry both blotted out and gave too much desperate importance to the lines. Far from the timeless absorption needed to bring a drawing through the portals of perception/invention. (In that slot, was present to see a new skein of snow-melt water appear in the long-dry sand of the wash. Heard it first, a rustling like a snake.)

So planned and thought and figured instead. Then gathered gear and kept walking, now with a mission of gathering things to paint at home. On up the main channel, finding a side canyon I hadn't noticed before, turning into it and immediately feeling that heightening of order—things suddenly look more "arranged", which of course they aren't; it's only my sense of design waking up. Followed bends of newly sandy wash, glimpsing mountain sheep up ahead. I'm hidden by a bend, then as I come out into the open again, ewe comes leaping across—big, thrusting, haunchy bounds. Sheep Leap Canyon? Then everything subsides into rapture. The perfect open bowl vainly sought in the other canyon, the perfect flat sandstone eyrie, my twelve stones laid out gleaming with significance in the last light. Wandered home (probably covered 7 or 8 miles that day) following a band of pinyon jays giving their quavery, querulous cries.

Volume 51 (*Chicago, Illinois, 1993*)

Oh rusty hand! Oh far away swooping across cornfields!

—the solid fountains of corn kernels auguring out of the combines, defiantly, extravagantly yellow.

—spewing of chewed-up silage, the prongs of the combines combing through standing corn, splayed fingers in disheveled hair.

—so many little dead bodies: kittens in front of farmhouses, raccoons crossing to cornfields, opossums crossing to thickets, groundhogs by grassy banks.

Drive across eastern Wyoming and into the new territory of western Nebraska. Dark embellishments of Pine Ridge and its attendant forms that ripple south from the Black Hills. Niobrara breaks, flowing grassland, strange remnant rock outcroppings. Reading Willa Cather's *Song of the Lark* as accompaniment to this trip.

Fort Robinson, its lush setting, ordered old ranks of buildings, absolutely deserted in late October, just cottonwood leaves blowing around in wan afternoon twiggy shadows. Spot where Crazy Horse was murdered "while resisting arrest". Bow to the six directions and become unhinged in time for awhile.

Terror of getting sucked into the spillway of traffic into Chicago—just rode with it in a stately manner, making only deliberate moves. Now safely docked in the Chicago Botanical Garden.

Volume 52 (*Wyoming, 1994*)

—July 23
Willow wickets
Hop-vines up the porch rails
Hummingbirds drinking deep
Heartening letters
Deep quiet
Few spoken words
Sleep during afternoon rain

Kittens in the garden
Slow clouds, no wind
Steady music on the inside
Worthy reading
Waiting in the garden
Summer dusk
Armloads of snapdragons
Scent of nicotiana opening in shadows
Nighthawks high up
Soft bleating from the goats
Sound of hose water on leaves of flowers

LAMAR VALLEY
August 12
Sun comes out briefly
at last moment
before dropping behind
mouth of the narrows
Distant hill becomes
rich and saturated
purple/violet

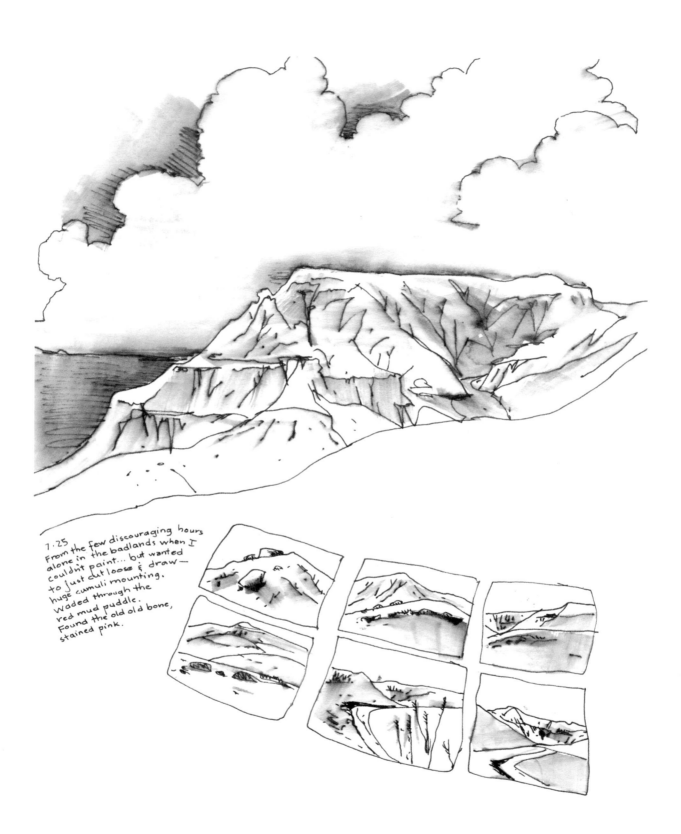

7.25
From the few discouraging hours
alone in the badlands when I
couldn't paint... but wanted
to just cut loose & draw—
huge cumuli mounting.
Waded through the
red mud puddle.
Found the old old bone,
stained pink.

Oct 26

To a remote snake R.
overlook — terrace
above, abandoned
channels again, crescent
shaped...

Watery, empty fields,
deep dun grass.
The north country
loneliness, abandonment.
A handful of quiet geese,
small ducks in a
backwater, one gull.
Rocks sliding occasion-
ally from the cliff
across the river.

C Notice different kinds of juniper:

low, spreading mat
pointed branchlets

this one extremely fine
& delicate, almost
creeping

this one has a more
upward, shrub-tending shape

These may be
different forms of
the same
species

outcrop of
limestone

Climb outcrop:
watching ants

several seem to be trying
to kill one - looks like same
species - one has grip by
antennae, one by leg
a third at thorax

B.
Mystery bird in aspens,
invisible, a buzzy scold
feeejh...feeejh

B

clumps of
bee balm...

potentilla or
shrubby cinquefoil?

aspens with juniper undergrowth

open hillside punctuated
with juniper mats and
single pines & spruces

A

camp

down to
the river
for nude
sunbathing

A.

— Young ruffed grouse (?)
explodes from
meadow

Meadow is grasses & forbs
harebell
yarrow
goldenrod
goatsbeard
yellow clover
cinquefoil

— Now I think this
is a sharp-tailed grouse

" If you would
know
aught,
be gay
before it."

could be no lovelier river....
flowing crystal over pure stone -
slanted bedrock and also a
cobbling of broken stones on
the bottom - dropping over
bedrock bars into whorling holes
Upriver, smooth dark water with
fiery glints on the riffles
Downriver warm stone color &
a hint of icy turquoise in
water....

Too many flies to stay nude...
walking & wading w/ only shirt
on, looking at caddis fly cases
and other under-stone larvae,
while swatting horseflies.
Two kinds of caddisflies so far:
The kind that
build little
stone
casings

& the kind that
build these
4-sided things
of I don't
know what
material.

Some of the stone-house
caddisflies are 2" long....

pink

green

yellow

Paintbrush-
like, only
bracts
are
half pink
&
half
green
and
more
rounded

Dipper
Swainson's thrush
Red Breasted nuthatch
Cedar waxwing
Townsend's solitaire
Nighthawk (L?)
Ruby crowned kinglet
Warbling vireo
Ruffed grouse?
Clark's nutcracker
Goldfinch
Pine Siskin
Flicker
Audubon's warbler
Sapsucker
A little flycatcher
w/ some yellow &
an apparently paler
tail border - by river

→ Cedar Waxwing,
flycatching!

190

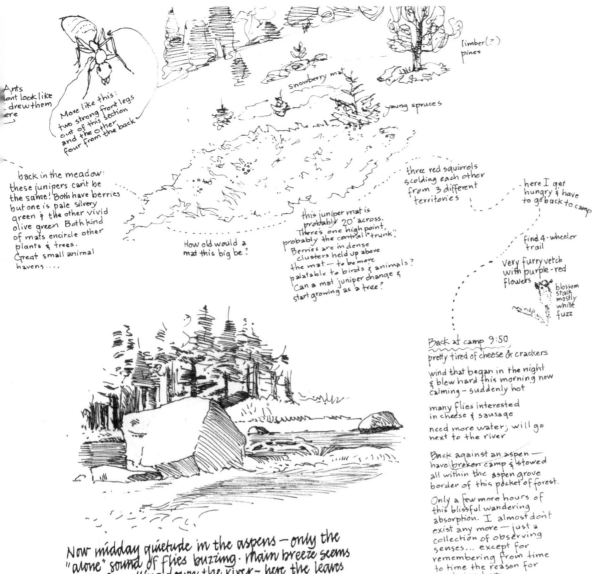

Ants
don't look like
I drew them
here

More like this:
two strong front legs
out of this section
and the other
four from the back

limber(?)
pines

Snowberry mat

young spruces

back in the meadow:
these junipers can't be
the same! Both have berries
but one is pale silvery
green & the other vivid
olive green. Both kind
of mats encircle other
plants & trees.
Great small animal
havens....

How old would a
mat this big be?

this juniper mat is
probably 20' across.
There's one high point,
probably the central "trunk".
Berries are in dense
clusters held up above
the mat — to be more
palatable to birds & animals?
Can a mat juniper change &
start growing as a tree?

three red squirrels
scolding each other
from 3 different
territories

here I get
hungry & have
to go back to camp

find 4-wheeler
trail

Very furry vetch
with purple-red
flowers

blossom
stalk
mostly
white
fuzz

Back at camp 9:50

pretty tired of cheese & crackers

wind that began in the night
& blew hard this morning now
calming — suddenly hot

many flies interested
in cheese & sausage

need more water; will go
next to the river

Back against an aspen —
have broken camp & stowed
all within the aspen grove
border of this pocket of forest.

Only a few more hours of
this blissful wandering
absorption. I almost don't
exist any more — just a
collection of observing
senses... except for
remembering from time
to time the reason for
my being here.

This is new territory for me —
northern Rockies, far from my
much higher & drier Wyoming
home. But my fate is clearly
bound up with this place
not only Dearborn country,
but the whole Front, the
prairie foothills, the potholes,
the shapes of peaks & buttes,
the reaches of grass hills.

Now midday quietude in the aspens — only the
"alone" sound of flies buzzing. Main breeze seems
to be funnelling down the river — here the leaves
tremble only slightly, without a sound. Far
from everything, but in the embrace of this
new "home". We toured Augusta briefly yesterday —
would like to get a better feel for the town — was
crowing over the shady streets & modest little houses
with their green lawns & thriving gardens. Not
"discovered," as in Dubois, but sense a small
community of devotees. Would be strange to
think of leaving Wyoming — but it could be
done..... still, only with much planning...
Legs & feet still feel cool from wading in the river.
Found a pile of (bear?) shit on the riverside stones
and stirred it up to serve as a fly lure — it worked.
Key may appear soon. Am going to drift, then
do an unencumbered hike....

191

C O L D   A. M.

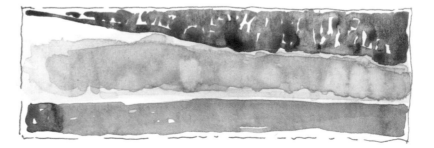

BROOKS LAKE
9 · 16

192

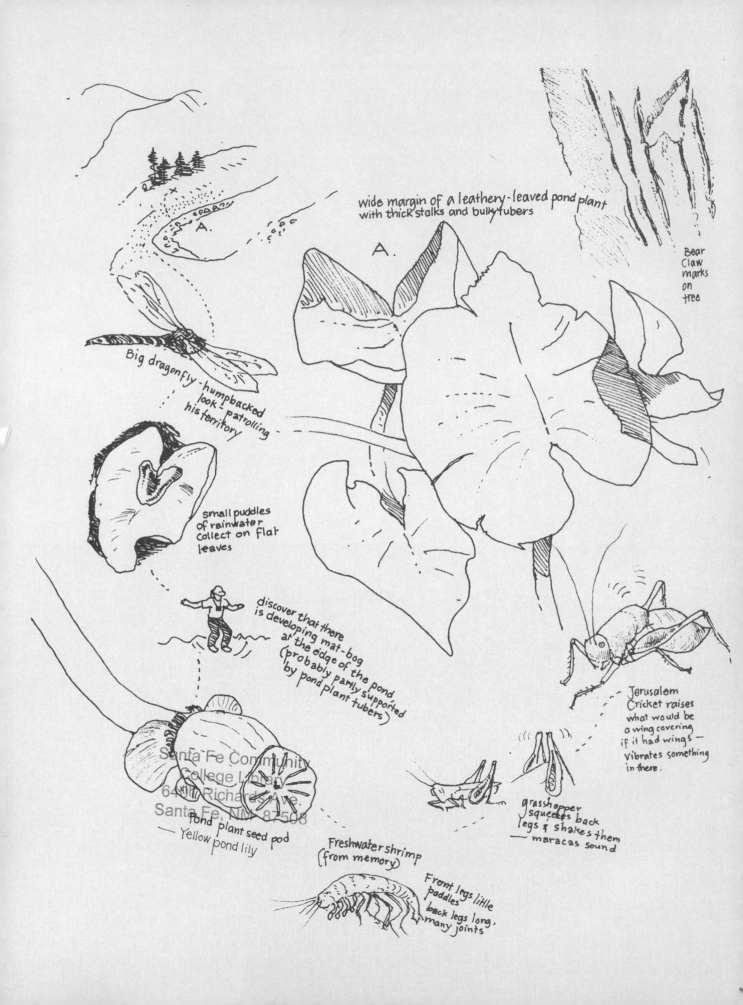

wide margin of a leathery-leaved pond plant with thick stalks and bulky tubers

A.

A.

Bear Claw marks on tree

Big dragonfly - humpbacked look - patrolling his territory

small puddles of rainwater collect on flat leaves

discover that there is developing mat-bog at the edge of the pond (probably partly supported by pond plant tubers)

pond plant seed pod — Yellow pond lily

Freshwater shrimp (from memory)

Front legs little paddles back legs long, many joints

Jerusalem Cricket raises what would be a wing covering if it had wings — vibrates something in there.

grasshopper squeezes back legs & shakes them — maracas sound